Reshaping the Mind

Reshaping the Mind

How Rationality can Provide Insights into the Feeling-self
and Other Minds

DAVID FRIEND

 **PETROC PRESS**

Petroc Press, an imprint of LibraPharm Limited

Distributors

Plymbridge Distributors Limited, Plymbridge House, Estover Road, Plymouth PL6 7PZ, UK

Published in the United Kingdom by LibraPharm Limited, *Gemini House*, 162 Craven Road, Newbury, Berkshire RG14 5NR, UK

A catalogue record for this book is available from the British Library

ISBN 1 900603 11 X

Typeset by Richard Powell Editorial and Production Services, Basingstoke, Hampshire RG22 4TX
Printed and bound in the United Kingdom by MPG Books Limited, Bodmin, Cornwall

Contents

Preface

My interest in the human nervous system began early, when, as a pharmacy student, I gravitated towards pharmacology. This leaning was reinforced when I joined the pharmaceutical industry and became involved with the leading general anaesthetic of its day and the launch of the world's first beta-blocker.

A formative step in my career occurred in the late 1960s when I lived in Japan for two years. I was able to observe an entirely different medical culture at first hand. It was here that the importance of the scientific method in evaluating new medicines became glaringly apparent, with the paramount need for statistically controlled studies. My interests became more global on returning to the UK and I was able to study a variety of medical cultures as the regulatory environment for the industry hardened, led by the Food and Drugs Administration in the United States.

When I entered the ranks of senior management my attention turned towards people, and I began to realise that not everybody thought like me. An industry like pharmaceuticals is inevitably influenced by its large research base and the army of doctors and scientists it employs. The resultant culture often came across as arrogant to colleagues in other businesses. We were even accused of rejecting outsiders who tried to make a late company move into the pharmaceuticals business.

The last seven years of my career were spent as chief executive of my company's international pharmaceuticals business. This gave me plenty of food for thought as I held the ring between centrist mandarins at business headquarters and independence movements in the operating units as they fought for more freedom to respond to local conditions – all this trapped within the organisational matrix of a large diversified company. I could not help but observe a fascinating mixture of mental repertoires; dramatised even further by inter-company politics during the two years I was president of the European pharmaceutical industry association.

As I neared the end of my career and thought about how to occupy myself during retirement, I decided I would try and give young professionals an insight into the human mind, which I wish I had had when I started my career. Of course, today we are in the middle of an explosion in cognitive science which wasn't around when I was young, so I have been digging in fertile ground. I hope this book is able to convey the flavour of the exhilarating times we live in.

Having spent my working career in industry I am the first to acknowledge the loneliness of the long-distance writer and the need for a little external help. This is especially true for someone who has no contact with other people who write books. It is therefore a special pleasure to acknowledge the help I received from those who were willing to read what I had written and to let me have their comments. Tom McKillop was the brave volunteer who read and provided valuable guidance on my first stumbling efforts and who even persuaded Liz McKillop to prepare a delicious meal to fortify me for the critical ordeal afterwards.

My second draft was read by several people, but it was the combination of views from Ben Green and Chris Petty which convinced me that a radical rewrite was necessary. Comments from both were taken on board. A potential route to publication had been identified by Bob Tomlinson before I decided on a rewrite, and 12 months later he pursued the matter of publication in a way which was enormously helpful. I had not intended to give my final manuscript to anyone to read, because at some point you have to decide to stop and take a chance with what you have, but I did ask my daughter, Susan, to read the Introduction. To my surprise she found it an easy read and settled down with the rest of the manuscript, running out of 'post-it' slips in the process of correcting the errors. My grateful thanks to all.

Finally, I would like to acknowledge Peter Clarke's help in taking on publication with such enthusiasm. The subject of mind is an inexhaustible one and I will continue to read avidly all I can lay my hands on. Whatever the reaction to this book, I hope it will turn up one or two interesting avenues to pursue. The *Journal of Consciousness Studies* and the various on-line Internet forums have been particularly important in giving me a sense of being up to date, though I am not able to compete with the resources of those in an academic setting. However, I do hope the rather unusual perspective I have adopted will stimulate a number of minds that might not otherwise have been interested in the subject of their own thought processes.

Macclesfield, May 1997   DF

Acknowledgements

The author and publishers acknowledge the following sources for granting permission to reproduce copyrighted material:

1. Times Newspapers Limited for the quotation at the foot of page 106 which originally appeared in *The Times*, July 19th, 1995 (© Times Newspapers Limited, 1995).
2. Macmillan General Books for the quotation on page 133 which originally appeared in Thorne, K. S. (1994). *Black Holes and Time Warps: Einstein's Outrageous Legacy*. London: Macmillan General Books.

Introduction

Other Minds

In one sense, people with successful careers are quite good at reading the minds of others. They have to be; otherwise how would they succeed in a competitive social environment? It is as well to have some idea of what the boss or the customer wants if you wish to prosper. But, as successful as they may be, most individuals are likely at some point to find themselves shocked or puzzled by the mental attitude of a colleague whose mind they thought they knew well. You may even be able to recall the last time this happened to you, especially if the episode resulted in consequences you regarded as unwelcome. Indeed, totally unexpected reactions can happen with a partner, spouse or best friend, even after a lifetime's acquaintance, as many can testify to from personal experience.

During a career in an international industry I observed a bewildering repertoire of mental attitudes, even though the community I worked in would be considered by some as boringly uniform. Beneath the exterior show of each of us there is a complex mixture of feelings, beliefs and desires which barely reach the surface and are known only to the individual concerned. Even then we may only be conscious of our own mental state in a vague sort of way because insight into our own mind is not profound and, at best, it is based on a rudimentary understanding of how the complex instrument we call a brain works. Through simple observation it is obvious that our thought processes are all different, but, because we can never enter another person's mind, there is an innate tendency to project our own values and thinking style on to others.

The Developing Mind

As children we learn to interpret the behaviour and words of others, and this gives us what is sometimes known as a *theory of mind*[1]. It first becomes apparent between the ages of three and four, interestingly when we are starting to acquire language, and it enables children to recognise what others want or believe in situations where there are fairly straightforward clues about what to expect. Development of this ability enables us as adults

1

to make a good guess about what others might be thinking and to predict
what they might say or do, often with notable success. We take this sort of
ability for granted, just as we do our ability to acquire language, but it only
takes us so far in being able to judge what is going on in another mind. At
the deeper level of feelings and beliefs we can get it badly wrong, because
we misattribute elements of our own outlook to others. Sometimes the brain
fails to develop the necessary circuitry for even the most basic understanding of how others are thinking, and a deficit becomes obvious. Such is
the case with *autism*, where children fail to acquire normal social skills and
are unable to interpret the behaviour of others. Autism might be regarded as
one extreme of the spectrum of mind reading ability, a sort of mindblindness[2], but it is a fairly safe assumption that mind reading prowess will
vary throughout the whole population. Most human characteristics do. Even
in the case of autism, and despite many years of study, no one has any real
idea of the specific brain pathology which underlies the condition. Such is
the elementary state of our knowledge about the brain.

Investigating the Mind

When we consider the mind there is a good deal of evidence to evaluate, but
even more theory. One illustration of this is the great mystery lying at the
centre of human experience – the nature of consciousness. Although there
are theories of how certain aspects of conscious experience may arise from
physical processes in the brain, there is precious little hard evidence to
guide us. We know that processes in the brain are related to the way billions
of nerve cells (neurons) connect up with one another and the firing patterns
they generate, but there are so many neurons that we are faced with the
daunting problem of an astronomical number of possible combinations.
Within the grey matter of our cerebral hemispheres – the cerebral cortex –
there are 10 billion or so neurons with a million billion connections between
them. This intricate structure is concentrated in a sheet of tissue about the
size of a large table napkin and no more than a few millimetres thick. The
neocortex is evolutionarily the most advanced part of the brain and it links
up with billions of neurons in other vital structures of the central nervous
system. The most important of these structures, for our purposes, are
identified in Chapter 1.

The task of investigating the behaviour of neurons falls to *neuroscientists*. They generally carry out their work in experimental animals and
so concentrate on functions which can be studied without the need for any

verbal report on the part of the subject. Memory and vision are two favourites. There are non-invasive, high-technology procedures which allow *neurologists* and *neuropsychologists* to investigate the human brain, but these cannot be applied at the level of individual neurons and their circuits. These techniques can give an indication of which areas of the brain are active during specific tasks, like visualising a scene or listening to music, so a better understanding of broad patterns of activity is gradually emerging. Incidents involving brain injury or surgical intervention can also provide important insights. Another approach is to build electronic networks using silicon chips and to try and simulate neural processes, but the level of complexity at which even the most advanced computers work is strikingly below that of the brain. Nevertheless, there are important lessons to be learned from the work of *cognitive scientists* applying themselves to artificial intelligence. The whole scene is surveyed by *philosophers of mind* who try to draw the threads together from the various scientific disciplines in order to weave their own theories of mind. As you can imagine, with the present state of knowledge, there are some dramatically opposing views about the way the human brain manages its conscious thought processes. Science cannot, at the moment, throw much light on how the brain copes with our higher cognitive processes involving reason and creativity.

Folk Psychology

All this suggests it may be a hopeless task trying to assess what is going on in the minds of other people, but if we are to make progress we need to assemble the essence of what is known about the brain and infuse it with the experience we can see all around us. This approach relies a lot on what is now known as *folk psychology* – a practical, common-sense approach towards properties of mind that we can observe in every-day life. Such properties include *beliefs*, *desires*, *feelings* and *thoughts*. Some philosophers would like to eliminate folk psychology and replace it with neuroscientific explanations of how the mind works, but that is likely to take a long time. One psychological property of especial interest is *rationality*, since it can be regarded as one of the higher functions of the human mind and it comes into play when we have to analyse complex situations and make judgements on a limited amount of evidence. Issues requiring rational evaluation confront people every day in large organisations, though emotional factors are often more influential in determining action. The interplay of emotional feelings and rationality within our thought processes, and how those thought processes arise within the brain, is something I find especially fascinating. Tackling such elusive issues means it will be necessary to examine mental processes at different levels, ranging between the intricate details of neuro-biology at the lowest level to facets of observable human behaviour at the other extreme. There has to be a lot of speculation in between. To illustrate my points on behaviour as trenchantly as possible I will revert to widely known historical episodes involving famous artists and inter-national statesmen, recognising that I am often using a good deal of licence in over-simplifying the events they were involved in, or the way their minds may have worked. My purpose is not to offer a superficial historical judgement, but to point up possible aspects of mind in an in-teresting way.

Complexity

As the brain is such an extraordinarily complex instrument, we have to bear in mind the effects of that complexity. When we are born there are well over 100 billion neurons in our brains, many of which are destined to become redundant and die. The synaptic connections between the 100 billion or so that survive are greatly influenced by the experience of the individual in early childhood, since those synaptic linkages used regularly tend to become strengthened and those that are unused wither. There is also a lot going on within each individual neuron. All cells are controlled by the active genes in their DNA and there are 30,000 genes[3] in the brain busily synthesising protein molecules for a whole range of purposes, many of which are poorly understood. Although the human genetic code lays down a basic plan for the brain, it is not a hard-wired plan like the design of a computer circuit. Much is left to chance and environmental influences. The brain can therefore be viewed as a self-organising *complex adaptive system* where elements of chaos theory apply. A feature of such systems is that there is a level of uncertainty about them, with outcomes from their activity predictable only on the basis of probability, i.e. any particular result cannot be calculated reliably and is therefore not 100% predictable. Think of what this means for a group of people witnessing the same event. No two people will exhibit the same degree of attention or process their perceptions in exactly the same way, and it is impossible to predict exactly how the neural pathways in their brains will behave. The more complex the event the more likely it is that they will end up with different mental experiences, even before emotions and memories programmed into their neural circuitry have exerted their modulating influence.

Subjectivity

When we consider the thoughts of others, or even our own thoughts, we have entered a non-spatial, subjective world where we cannot apply the usual procedures of science in observing what is going on. Science is unable to provide us with an adequate analysis of the conscious mind at the present time, and some philosophers doubt that it ever will[4]. This relates to the fact that science depends for its results on objective investigation which, as far as possible, eliminates subjective bias. To do this it often employs mathematical and statistical techniques. How can we employ such an approach with the mind when the essence of our insights is subjective? My sensations, associated with vibrant autumnal colours, bleak mountain scenery, a ravishing Schubert melody, or a boring television soap, are peculiarly my own. Notice the loaded adjectives I have used to reflect my attitude, which it would not be appropriate to apply to many other minds. If such responses are largely emotional and individual, is there any way of making an objective assessment about such every-day perceptions? To a degree there is, though it is not always easy to pin down or to capture at the level of the individual. To reach a useful result we have to take into account the effects of *time*, *algorithmic* processes, and the *statistical* results they generate. After explaining what I mean by these terms, I will illustrate them with some examples from experience of the world around us.

Algorithms and Related Things

An algorithm is a procedure used to calculate an answer and it provides the standard technique for programming digital computers. I would like to use it in a much wider context than that since there does not appear to be an alternative word to suit my purpose. That much of the brain's activity is algorithmic is envisaged by Roger Penrose, even though he has written at great length arguing that consciousness in human beings is ultimately non-algorithmic[5]. Whether a conscious computer is theoretically possible remains an open question. The essential point about an algorithm is that it is its own shortest description, and cannot be compressed. There is no way of predicting what an algorithm will do other than to execute it and observe what emerges[6]. We have already seen that it is impossible to calculate the outcome from complex systems which behave in a chaotic manner because we cannot define the initial conditions or the processing they undergo with sufficient accuracy. The only thing that can provide the answer is the system itself after it has run its due course. It runs its own algorithm over the time it takes to reach its changed state and there is no shorter way of achieving an answer. Statistical predictions can, of course, be made and we see this done regularly in weather forecasting, with various degrees of success. Economists also try to predict economic systems, though with rather less success. Part of the reason for this is the time scale involved. Even the most super of super-computers cannot help us much with the weather three months ahead. To differentiate the way I am going to use the word 'algorithm' from a 'rule' which can be used to calculate an answer, I will prefix it with the word *emergent* and use the two words together in hyphenated form. An *emergent-algorithm*, then, is one that can only emerge from the system or process being considered. I hope the following examples will make my usage clear.

The Judgement of History

Let's consider the case of Johann Sebastian Bach, who is now considered by some musical authorities to be the most technically accomplished composer who ever lived. It would be hard to maintain that his genius was fully recognised in his day. When he was appointed, quite late in his career, to his position in Leipzig, he was third choice behind Telemann and Graupner. Graupner? Bach's music went largely unrecognised for 100 years after his death until revived by Mendelssohn and others. Although views today will vary on his precise ranking among the great composers, virtually everyone will have him in their first team. Why wasn't Bach's genius recognised immediately? To answer that all you have to do is try and identify the Bach among today's composers. The verdict of society cannot be reached with confidence until there have been countless interactions and iterations of individual judgements, a process which takes time and can be regarded as an emergent-algorithm. Many knife-edged decisions have to be made, which can go one way or another. The statistical outcome and the pattern it generates is a product of numerous minds, but it is impossible for any one mind to predict the result reliably.

The verdict on Bach may now seem pretty obvious because of his technical prowess and enormous output, but how about Jane Austen with her six, rather simple, country novels? She did not exhibit the command of language displayed by Dickens, the productivity of Trollope, or the intellectual style of George Eliot. Yet, the judgement of history is that she was one of the great 19th century novelists. How many tortuous twists and turns did her reputation have to go through before that verdict could be pronounced with confidence on her rather sparse output, while the work of many of her contemporaries was forgotten? Which of today's novelists will be read in 200 years' time? We can all make our individual guesses but the probability of getting it right is little better than chance because the procedure required to generate the answer – the historical emergent-algorithm – takes time and cannot be compressed. In the end the verdict on Jane Austen, or anyone else, is a statistical one which may change as values and ideas change, so we can never say we have arrived at a definitive conclusion.

The 19th century also gives us an interesting example in the field of politics. Abraham Lincoln and William Gladstone were exact contemporaries, both being born in 1809. Gladstone obtained a double first at Oxford, became a great orator and had vast stores of energy. He led the greatest power of his day over four administrations and was held in awe by many of his contemporaries. He was probably the cleverest Prime Minister Great Britain ever had. Lincoln was largely self-educated and he lived far away from the polished societies of European civilisation. Many doubts were expressed about his abilities during his first term of office as President and his conduct of the civil war was heavily criticised by contemporaries. He was assassinated at the beginning of his second administration, before the surrender terms for the South were cut and dried. It was his actions and words which were to ring through history as he laid the foundations for the United States to emerge as the leading 20th century power. Gladstone spent years trying to resolve Ireland's difficulties without success and was destined for a secondary role on the historical world stage. What odds in 1862 on this rational judgement of history?

The Collective Mind

While we have to wait a long time to determine the heights of human achievement, we can observe the algorithmic process at work on a much shorter time scale in the market place or in any large organisation. A company bringing a new product to market does so in the expectation that it will achieve a certain degree of success, though it realises it will be the collective judgement of customers which will determine the eventual outcome. That process may take a year or two, but once again we have an objective result from a lot of subjective, individual decisions. The 'invisible hand' of the market place makes a rational assessment about the product. A crisper insight into the collective mind can perhaps be achieved by looking at some of the processes within a company, because here there is a formal organisational structure which brings people into contact with one another in order to get a product to market. Research, development, production and marketing are all essential activities which have to be co-ordinated and brought together through interdisciplinary teams. No one person can solve all the problems that have to be solved and the organisation eventually develops a consensus view about the right way to go. The way this is done gives each company its individual character; its 'collective mind'. The interesting thing about this collective mind is that it has to behave rationally, or at least it should do if it wants to get good results. It has to weigh facts and opinions, risks and probabilities, in as objective a manner as possible. If it doesn't it will lose out to its competitors and survival will be put at risk. This doesn't mean to say there isn't a good deal of emotion generated within most companies, merely that, in the end, it gets balanced out. When companies do fail it can be ultimately analysed as a failure of rationality.

The Individual Mind

Just as a company or a government comes to a decision after a good deal of intercommunication and iteration, so, it can be argued, does the brain. The number of people in any organisation is trivial compared with the number of neurons in the brain, yet individual neurons have a role in what we think about and what we are conscious of. On that there is general agreement. There are some authorities who believe that sub-neuronal processes involving quantum gravity effects have a place in generating conscious experience, but such ideas are controversial and impossible to prove or disprove at the present time. It can also be argued that the highly complex chemistry of living cells has something to do with conscious thought processes, which is obviously true because dead cells are not of much use. But it would seem to be the wrong level for analysing how the brain works, just as looking at individual neurons would not tell us much about the judgements of history or how organisations work. When we look at the mind we can think of it as an immensely complicated computer with millions of billions of connections. But that could be misleading. A computer is a digital machine which operates on the basis of bits of information which it can manipulate with a high level of reproducibility. The brain relies on analogue processing of disparate inputs, and the interactions of neuronal networks could have more in common with the chaotic emergent-algorithms of human society than the precise programs of computers. There is a type of computer architecture which does process analogue information in a highly parallel way and which is designed to simulate neuronal networks more realistically than the serial computer programs we are all familiar with. This has given rise to a school of computational neuroscience known as *connectionism*, and it has achieved some notable successes in mimicking simple aspects of sensory and motor performance of animal nervous systems.

Our sensory apparatus depends on a number of transducers which convert external energy into neuronal energy. These are the rods and cones of the retina of the eye, the hair cells in the cochlea of the ear, and the touch receptors in the skin. Our brains are constantly bombarded by sensory experiences which arrive in random fashion and from which order must be constructed so that a state of conscious awareness can be achieved. No computer, even a parallel one, has yet been designed which can even approach these operations in anything like a convincing manner. Whether one ever will remains a matter of speculation. Even if we regard the brain as an information processing machine we cannot for one moment view it as a specially designed organ for human beings. That would disregard all the tenets of Darwinian evolution. Our brains exhibit structures that have been inherited from more lowly creatures and on top of which more advanced structures have evolved. The emotional centres of our brains bear strong similarity to the emotional centres of our forebears, and these can still be a dominating influence in our lives. When we consider the higher, rational systems in the brain we have to realise that the effective operation of these systems is greatly dependent on nourishment of the emotional centres, since it is they which eventually make our decisions.

Rationality in Perspective

When, during the course of this book, I look at patterns of rationality in the human mind I would not like you to think for one moment that I am underestimating the importance of emotion. What I am trying to do is to draw up a balance between rationality and emotion and to make a guess where the future will take us. As I have indicated earlier, my guess is likely to be no better than chance in predicting the right result, and it is only the emergent-algorithm of cultural evolution which will provide the answer. Nevertheless, I hope you will agree it is worthwhile exploring the possibilities. Given the emotional needs that we all have, it is easy to satirise the application of, what appears to be, cold blooded rationality, as Charles Dickens did nearly a century and a half ago in *Hard Times* with his portrait of Thomas Gradgrind and his obsession with facts:

'In this life, we want nothing but Facts, sir; nothing but Facts!'

But, on reflection, this can be diagnosed as an extremely irrational position, because it is demonstrably untrue as a statement about the needs of any one of us, and Gradgrind's failures within his family hardly come as a surprise. In emphasising rationality in this account of the human mind I am not trying to make it a remedy for every ill. However complicated our lives become, I hope there will always be a place for pure, irrational happiness. I can never see rationality becoming an essential part of the recipe for joy, but it could have a formative influence on the evolution of human culture.

Chapter 1

Some Insights into the Brain

Brain and Mind

Before we can proceed we really need to develop a point of view about the brain, as our organ of emotion and rationality. This is no easy task and it is bound to involve us in some controversy, since different views abound on the way the brain, and the mind it operates, can be interpreted. Perhaps this is the first point on which to reach some agreement – are 'mind' and 'brain' elements of the same thing? The way we answer this question will depend on whether we are materialists or dualists, whether we believe everything can be explained by biology, chemistry and physics, or whether we hold there is some element outside the domains of these sciences which accounts for vital characteristics of the human mind. There is no absence of scope for different interpretations. Everyone will agree that there are many things which science cannot explain at the present time, but the question is whether it will have the capability eventually to unravel the deepest mysteries of mind. My own tentative position is that there are probably neurophysiological explanations for everything which goes on in the mind, but the sheer scale of mathematical possibilities involved may defeat mankind in discovering the fundamental truths. We can theorise and speculate endlessly, but we will eventually be judged in what we say on the evidence which supports our views. Belief, in the absence of evidence, may be something which is of inestimable value in our personal lives, but this does not mean it will stand up well in the context of historical judgement on matters of fact.

Philosophical Foundations

Speculation about the nature of mind has been within the natural realm of philosophy since the dawn of civilisation, being more in fashion sometimes than others. Today, the subject is at the forefront of philosophical discourse, largely, I suspect, because of the activity of the sciences on which philosophical views can be based. Such philosophical speculation is of great value in teasing out the issues, but it can only produce definitive answers on the mind if those answers are supported by the evidence. That evidence is provided by scientific enquiry, and without it we remain in the realms of circular debate. Perhaps one of the most startling things about philosophy is the spread of views that exists, many of them in direct conflict with one another. There are, of course, conflicts of view in science, but there tends to be convergence over time. This does not appear to be true of philosophy, unless it has the help of science, but scientific evidence on the mind is in such a rudimentary state that it still allows room for great divides within philosophical opinion.

Inevitably, the development of computers has had a great influence on the debate. *Functionalist* philosophers believe the mind is a computer of sorts but they are not always able to agree on what sort of computer. The digital computers we are all familiar with are serial machines which process a set of coded representations according to algorithmic rules laid down in a piece of software – the program. But there are other highly parallel computers which do not need a program at all and which develop their outputs by a process of adjusting the weights of their connections – resulting in a field of cognitive science known as *connectionism*[1]. Since the operation of our brains depends on billions of parallel neural pathways and the strength of their synaptic connections, 'connectionism' can be seen as a more realistic way of representing the brain's operations. There is certainly biological evidence that neuronal networks do become strengthened with repeated stimulation – an observation made nearly 50 years ago by a Canadian neurophysiologist, Donald Hebb[2]. Consequently, networks which operate in this way, whether assemblies of neurons or artificial circuits, are often referred to as *Hebbian*. Modern neuroscientists have extended Hebb's concept to talk about more complex arrangements of neurons, using terms like 're-entrant maps', 'recurrent networks', 'reverberant loops', where there is a persistent recycling of neuronal signals to serve as the agency by which we develop our thought processes. The way the brain encodes its representations of the world in our thoughts is a matter for much speculation, the *classical* school of functionalist philosophers maintaining there is a 'language of thought' which the brain processes in specialised modules, and the *connectionist* school maintaining there is no fundamental role for language, the essential element being synaptic weight configurations and the vectorial patterns they generate. Whatever our mode of thinking, there is no doubt our thoughts have to be translated into language for us to communicate with each other, and composing sentences in English, or any other natural language, feels much like a serial process. The last word in the debate is a long way off.

There are yet other strongly held views that the brain does not operate like a computer at all, an opinion shared by a number of philosophers, neuroscientists, and even mathematicians interested in the brain. None of these thinkers believes that there is any supernatural or spiritual element associated with conscious processes, but their naturalistic explanations for human mental experience tend to differ. They range from the top-down proposition that the neurophysiology of the brain exhibits *emergent* properties (the character of the whole adds up to something greater than the sum of the individual parts) to the bottom-up idea that the underlying microstructure of neurons can give rise to quantum mechanical effects which generate consciousness. None of these differences in theoretical outlook can be resolved by looking at the evidence, so there is still room for holding dualistic beliefs and retaining faith in the existence of an immortal soul as the basis of human consciousness. It has to be said that, among philosophers and cognitive scientists, dualistic interpretations of mind are in a distinctly minority position. Where, then, does this leave us in gaining some insight into the brain? I propose we proceed on the basis of what can be established as factual, with a reasonable degree of confidence, and use that as a springboard for a working hypothesis.

The Developing Mind

We know that at two years old our brains have more neurons and more synaptic connections than they have at any stage during the rest of our lives[3]. By the time we reach maturity we can have lost 50% of neuronal synapses. Yet, as young children memory and self-awareness are undeveloped. Genetic inheritance has determined the basic design of our brains, but there is obviously something not yet in place. The conclusion that development of our mind is dependent on the sensory experiences it undergoes is inescapable. The effects that the absence of normal experience can produce is illustrated by those tragic cases where children have been deprived of contact with the outside world because of the actions of a deranged parent. There is retardation in mental development and a handicap in using language which can never be entirely overcome once the brain has reached a certain level of maturity. Work with animals has consistently demonstrated that experience during their growth phase is critical in determining their behaviour as adults. In one instance, when a group of Scottish terriers was deprived of normal sensory experience during rearing, the individuals became untrainable and abnormal in personality and social behaviour[4]. One animal was so unable to learn from painful experiences that he kept sticking his nose into a lighted cigar. All the evidence points in the direction that learning during the early years of growth has a crucial impact on the nature of the adult's mental processes. Obviously, our minds are not determined entirely by the way we are nurtured. The genetic component is just as important. We only have to consider the case of autistic children to make the point. There is a deficit somewhere in the structure of their brain which cannot be fully overcome with training, so that they always have difficulty in appreciating how other people think. Experience can only build on what is there.

Gerald Edelman is one eminent neuroscientist who has written at length about the development of the brain[5]. He is very clear that it is not a structure with fixed wiring but is organised with populations of neurons being selected for particular activities over time; a process he has called neural Darwinism. Those population groups which get used are strengthened, and those which don't, wither. Maps are created in the brain for particular activities, and it is the re-entrance of signals into these maps which evokes memory. Many neuroscientists would agree with this basic view, though they may well prefer different terminology. This does not mean our brains lack a common structure. They have specialised areas which we all share, just as my hands have the same basic anatomical features as those of a concert pianist. The muscle fibres and their nerve connections in my fingers, however, may have developed rather differently. We cannot use invasive techniques on human beings to actually confirm what is happening to neuronal circuits. Even in experimental animals scientists can only use a small number of microelectrodes at a time. Monitoring a thousand neurons would be a trivial number in terms of the brain's activity, but any live animal would be dead before all those electrodes could be inserted. Non-invasive techniques are being used increasingly, but they can only indicate broad bands of activity.

The knowledge we have of the brain enables us to paint the following picture of the development of our mental processes. Our genetic inheritance provides us with a central nervous system structured to interpret what we see and hear and the ability to convert our thoughts into language. The manner in which we are reared has a crucial impact on the way in which our sensory, motor and cognitive functions accomplish their tasks. Our early years of growth constitute the most sensitive period for laying down basic abilities, and neglect during these years will result in life-long shortfall against genetic potential. Although our brains all have the same basic structure, the neuronal circuits connecting one part of the brain to another are influenced by our experience, because repeated use strengthens and disuse weakens. The way we perceive the world depends on the character of our neuronal circuits, which have been determined in a large measure by our own individual experience as a human being. Since we have bespoke minds we can never truly appreciate what it feels like to be someone else, and no two individuals experience events in quite the same way. The emergent-algorithm of development which makes us what we are is so complex that there is virtually no chance of ever finding an exact duplicate of ourselves – we are forever unique. But, there is another important conclusion which emerges if all this is true. The functioning of our brains is, to a significant extent, determined by the society in which we are reared. The way we carry out mathematical calculations, form moral judgements and construct our beliefs is determined by how experience teaches us to embed memories and emotional responses in our neuronal circuitry, and relate them to one another. If the disciplines of learning change then the characteristics of society will change in a statistically measurable manner. Anyone who has memories of the last 50 years will be in no doubt about this.

Structure of the Brain

We should now turn to the daunting matter of neuroanatomy in order to obtain an impression of the brain which will help us in thinking about the mind. The brain is such a hideously complex organ that any brief description is bound to open itself up to charges of oversimplification, but I will have to risk that. All we need for our purposes is a working model which helps us visualise what is going on in a reasonably faithful manner. Fortunately, I am helped in this task by a description provided by Alexandr Luria, a renowned Russian neuropsychologist, who divided the cognitive centres of the brain into three blocks in one of his classical texts[6]. (This description omits the lower brain stem (or hind brain) controlling vital functions and muscular co-ordination.) Figure 1 illustrates these blocks, which I will describe as:

1. Subcortex [Luria's Block One)
2. Sensory cortex [Luria's Block Two)
3. Frontal cortex [Luria's Block Three)

In my use of the term *subcortex* I will not be strictly correct in neuroanatomical terms because I will be including parts of the basal cortex which belong to the cerebral hemispheres. These deep, inner areas of grey matter in the cerebral hemispheres have a close functional relationship with the evolutionarily older parts of the brain in the subcortex proper. Neuroscientists nowadays tend to use the terms *cortex* and *neocortex* interchangeably, and when I refer to *sensory cortex* and *frontal cortex* I will be talking about neocortex. The *neocortex* is the outer, grey matter of the brain which can be seen when viewing an intact brain. It is that convoluted outer sheet of the cerebral cortices which contains the cell bodies of neurones, and which is particularly well developed in man.

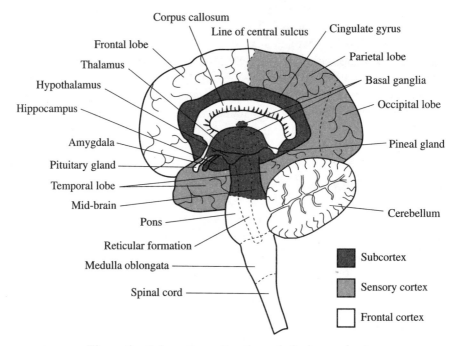

Figure 1   *Schematic section through the human brain*

The brain exhibits bilateral symmetry, so that although its structures are usually referred to in the singular there are generally two of them, or two lobes or tracks, as in the case of the left and right cerebral cortices. This applies equally to subcortical structures. Figure 1 is a schematic diagram which shows the brain regions I will be referring to. Though they are not all strictly in the same plane, the diagram does provide me with a useful picture of the structures and their relationship, so I hope the same will be true for you.

Subcortex

The subcortex influences much of our conscious activity by controlling our state of attention and arousal. Huge chunks of the neocortex can be removed without loss of consciousness, but if there is bilateral damage to vital parts of the thalamus or reticular formation in the midbrain, unconsciousness results. The main divisions of the subcortex are the thalamus, basal ganglia and limbic system, but these can be further subdivided into nuclei which all have their own special functions. To complete the picture we have to add the mid-brain reticular formation. The next thing we find is that everything is connected to everything else so that it is difficult to be sure about the precise functions of any one part. A simple, indicative picture will suffice for our purpose.

At the centre of the subcortex is the *thalamus*, which is an egg-shaped structure embedded deep in the heart of the brain. It acts as a receiving station for all sensory inputs with the exception of olfaction (smell), where signals go straight to the olfactory bulb. Visual and auditory signals are processed by dedicated nuclei (areas of grey matter) in the thalamus before being transmitted onwards by 'ascending' neuronal connections to the visual and auditory regions of the *sensory cortex*. Interestingly, neuronal connections 'descending' from the cortex to the thalamus far outnumber ascending connections. This suggests there is a lot of feedback and that signals are actively processed rather than simply relayed. We can envisage reverberating loops of neuronal activity between thalamus and cortex. In conjunction with the reticular formation, the thalamus tones up and energises the rest of the brain, so it has a crucial role in determining whether we are conscious or unconscious. The neuronal firing pattern it generates may well have an important role in binding together all the coded sensory impulses that the cortex has to deal with. A number of investigators have suggested this may be achieved through 40 Hz oscillations generated by neuronal action potentials in the intralaminar nucleus (ILN) of the thalamus.

Surrounding and overhanging the thalamus are the *basal ganglia*. This group of structures has direct connections to the frontal cortex and has a special role in motor activity. These nuclei also have extensive projections to the thalamus. The basal ganglia can be viewed as a motor operations centre which receives its commands from the executive centres in the frontal lobes. But it can also achieve a degree of independence from the neocortex because it takes control of well-practised muscular actions and relieves them of the need for rather slow conscious processes. This becomes apparent in driving a car or achieving proficiency in a game, such as tennis, where the automatic responses required are too fast for conscious deliberation. When a deficiency occurs in the predominant neurotransmitter (dopamine) employed in the basal ganglia, Parkinson's disease can result. Muscle co-ordination becomes very difficult because the sufferer finds that 'willed' commands from the cortex do not get translated into the required muscular action. Although people affected in this way are unable to will their arm to lift a tennis racket they can still respond with a smooth, flowing stroke if a tennis ball is thrown to them. A nucleus in the basal ganglia has implemented an automatic response laid down during earlier learning.

The *limbic system* encircles the thalamus and basal ganglia. It has a number of discrete structures, including the hypothalamus, hippocampus and amygdala. The grey matter in the lower, inner borders of the cerebral hemispheres (*limbus* means border) is also included. This area is known as the *cingulate gyrus*. The limbic system controls much of our memories and emotions. The *hypothalamus*, as its name implies, is located just under the thalamus. It weighs about 4 g and regulates a host of functions, including body temperature, hunger, thirst, sexual activity, the endocrine glands and various aspects of behaviour. This mere 4 g has a lot to do with our pleasure and our pain. But, like most areas of the brain, it does not act by itself. Its activity can be triggered by conscious thoughts and it, in turn, may then activate the autonomic nervous system, or the endocrine system via the *pituitary gland*. We have all experienced the vicious circle that this can create with anxious thoughts causing the hypothalamus to activate the sympathetic nervous system, resulting in increased heart rate and muscle tremor, which in turn cause further anxious thoughts. This is why it is necessary to include the autonomic nervous system (of which the sympathetic system is a part) in our considerations. Whenever we use an example like this it is important to remember that nothing is ever simple in the brain and numerous other pathways will be activated differently in different people. One person's racing heart is another person's gastric pain. But the hypothalamus is not concerned just with unpleasant experiences. An electrode planted in a certain part of the rat's hypothalamus will cause it to press a lever that delivers a pleasant stimulus, and it finds that stimulus so rewarding that it will keep on pressing that lever to the neglect of eating and drinking.

The part of the brain particularly associated with memory is the *hippocampus*. Numerous studies have been carried out in experimental animals to confirm that synaptic changes occur in the terminal endings of hippocampal neurons when memories are laid down. The changes that have been observed at the synaptic level involve sproutings in the cytoskeleton of axons and dendrites, resulting in long-lasting effects on neuronal firing patterns. We also know that damage to the hippocampus and associated areas (e.g. in Korsakoff's syndrome) can result in severe loss of memory. The hippocampus appears to have a role in orchestrating memory circuits in the cerebral cortex, and its links to the rest of the limbic system ensure that emotions play a large part in what we remember. There are substantial connections with the basal ganglia and thalamus, so some neuroscientists believe that the hippocampus is at the centre of a cognitive mapping system which allows comparisons to be made between sensory experience, memory and the emotions they evoke.

The *amygdala* is best thought of as the emotional core of the limbic system. It is particularly associated with powerful emotions like fear, anger and anxiety. Its connections to the hippocampus ensure that it has a role in the establishment of emotional memories and its links to the hypothalamus give it access to the autonomic nervous system and the effects it can produce in our bodies. Passionate and impulsive feelings generated in the amygdala and associated subcortical structures quite often override rational deliberations in the higher cortical centres and so the links between the two are obviously of vital importance.

Although there is good evidence for associating particular aspects of mental activity with the different subcortical structures, the divisions are not clear cut and the multiplicity of connections means that many different centres will be involved even in the simplest activities. For our purpose it is convenient to think of the subcortex as a unit: the essential dynamo to the brain, charging it up and initiating many of its automatic, subconscious responses. The subcortex comes into its own in well-rehearsed reactions or in crisis situations when actions have to take place before we can consciously evaluate them. It may be a matter of survival. If a mother sees one of her children in danger she will react immediately. Sensory processing in the thalamus will go directly to the basal ganglia for activating the necessary muscular response. The amygdala and the hypothalamus will produce a tremendous adrenergic surge throughout the body, increasing heart rate and blood supply to the muscles. There is likely to be an extreme emotional response and the memory of the occasion will become indelibly imprinted on the brain so that any repeat threat can be recognised instantly. It is not difficult to see the value of such a system, and it is one we share with many other animals. Because it is has such well-established evolutionary roots and is so potent in its effects it can disrupt operations in the higher centres, particularly in the frontal cortex where working memory is laid down. We become conscious of being unable to think clearly and our sensory experience may become distorted. It is a system crucial to our well being, but it is one that can also have undesirable effects if its powers are applied in inappropriate situations. We have to try and retain the right balance between our emotional centres and our rational centres. The cerebral cortex is particularly important for self-control and restraint, and the consequences of removing its influence can readily be seen if too much alcohol is consumed. Alcohol exerts its earliest effects on the higher centres.

Sensory Cortex

This sensory centre of the brain processes the information we receive from the outside world and from our own bodies. It occupies the occipital, parietal and temporal lobes in the posterior two-thirds of the cerebral hemispheres. The remaining one third, the frontal lobe, we will address separately. The primary visual cortex is located in the occipital lobe right at the back of the brain, and the auditory centres are found in the upper part of the temporal lobe. Nerve impulses related to sensations of pain, temperature, touch and pressure enter the parietal lobe just behind the central sulcus (the cleft which divides the parietal lobe from the frontal lobe). The processing and integration of these senses is not well understood but it is known that millions of neurons are involved in 'association' areas of the cortex located in the temporal and parietal lobes.

There is also a division of functions between the left and right hemispheres, with our powers to understand language residing in the left temporal lobe. The right temporal lobe is more concerned with spatial concepts and our body image. The precise location of functions will vary from individual to individual (for instance, some left-handed people have language located in the right hemisphere), so there is no hard and fast rule. The brain is a very 'plastic' organ with a high degree of what is known as *degeneracy* – if one part fails to take up a designated function during the critical years of development, then another one will. It would also be wrong to draw too tight a line on the functions of the different lobes, but it is quite useful to have a schematic picture. Some useful insights into brain function can be obtained when there is injury that causes loss of a particular ability or an abnormality, and so it is worth briefly considering some of these.

Right hemisphere lesions due to stroke or tumour give rise to a number of quite remarkable abnormalities of perception. Damage to the somatosensory area in the right parietal cortex and its connections with the thalamus, basal ganglia and frontal cortex can give rise to a condition known as *anosognosia*. The injury results in paralysis of the left side of the body but subjects are totally unaware of their injury or their incapacity. They believe they can still use both hands normally, despite evidence to the contrary. *Hemineglect* is a related condition where right parietal damage causes patients to totally ignore the left side of their body and to, in fact, disown it. Damage to the left side of the brain does not cause similar distortions in perception and this strongly suggests the dominant role of the right cortex in providing an integrated map of the body. But it isn't just with our own bodies that sensory functions go awry. *Prosopagnosia* is the inability to recognise the faces of other people, and this is often associated with a right hemisphere lesion. A famous example has been described by Oliver Sacks in *The Man who Mistook his Wife for a Hat*[7].

When there is injury to the left side of the brain there can be problems with language, resulting in *aphasia*. Damage to an area in the left temporal lobe, called Wernicke's area, causes difficulties with understanding speech. Problems in a related area in the left frontal lobe (Broca's area) cause difficulties in the production of speech (Broca's aphasia). It is worth noting that speaking, as a motor function, is located in the frontal cortex, and understanding speech in the sensory cortex. This helps to emphasise the division of activity between sensory and motor areas, but, as with most parts of the brain, there are overlaps and extensive interconnecting loops. Our picture of the world is put together in the sensory cortex, where memory circuits are established. Brain scanning techniques have shown that the same areas are active when we employ our memories in visualising a scene as were engaged when we first perceived the scene. Although there is a division of function between right and left brains there is generally seamless communication between the two hemispheres, because they are connected by a mass of fibres called the *corpus callosum*. If the corpus callosum is severed by surgical operation (commissurotomy) to treat certain cases of severe epilepsy, patients develop *split brain syndrome* where they are unable to name objects seen only in their left visual field. The signal going to their right hemisphere cannot be transmitted to the left hemisphere – the one concerned with language.

Our coherent, unified experiences of the world are dependent on the 'binding' of different sensory signals assembled by millions of neurons in operational areas of the sensory cortex. What we are conscious of seeing and hearing is the result of immensely complex neuronal firing patterns occupying large tracts of brain space. Neuroscientists studying senses in experimental animals have failed to detect any repeatable patterns in the brain associated with particular sensory experiences. This suggests that what we see and hear is dependent on neuronal patterns already laid down by our earlier experiences. If this is true it means each of us puts our per-ceptions together in a different manner because we all have different life histories. No outside observer will ever be able to read our thoughts because the algorithm emerging in any particular brain is uninterpretable except by the individual concerned. We should all find this reassuring.

Frontal Cortex

The frontal cortex does not receive or process information from the physical world and is linked externally through the sensory cortex. It does have direct connections to various nuclei in the subcortex, through which it initiates and orchestrates conscious motor activity and influences emotional behaviour. Muscles in the body are represented in great detail on the motor cortex of the frontal lobes, located just in front of the central sulcus, and this is sometimes referred to as the 'motor homunculus'. Broca's area has already been mentioned as the motor area of the frontal lobes associated with speech. The most forward area of the frontal cortex, known as the *prefrontal cortex*, enables us to undertake some of our most advanced behaviour, including the ability to plan for the future, to determine the course of our own actions and to achieve lasting intentions. This region has a special association with certain types of memory, particularly working memory, which we will discuss shortly. The prefrontal cortex enables us to examine our own shortcomings, and it gives us our sense of self. Development of this executive area of the brain is the feature which most distinguishes human beings from their ancestors on the evolutionary scale.

The subtle but vital role of the prefrontal cortex can be illustrated with the classical case of Phineas Gage. He was the foreman of a gang working on railways in the United States in the 1840s and he suffered an accident with an iron tamping rod when an explosive charge went off prematurely. The rod shot through the frontal area of his brain, but the damage was confined to the ventromedial area of the prefrontal cortex. Although he survived and remained physically active his personality changed dramatically. He was no longer able to make rational decisions about his future and his emotional behaviour became bizarre. It was as though his control system had been knocked out. Similar syndromes have been observed in other patients where prefrontal lobe damage has been diagnosed using modern neuropsychological techniques.

Many investigators who are willing to theorise on the basis of the limited evidence available attribute a central role to the prefrontal cortex in determining higher-level cognitive functions. There is ample proof that this region of the brain is not required for consciousness; after all, prefrontal lobotomy used to be carried out as a surgical procedure for serious mental disease. But the effects of this procedure on the quality and content of conscious experience now make it unacceptable. The role of the prefrontal cortex in the control of different types of memory (working, episodic and emotional) would alone ensure that it has a crucial place in the finer aspects of intellectual activity, but it is also fairly certain that it influences the way we reach our judgements and organise our rational processes. There are obvious difficulties in investigating higher order neurophysiological functions found only in human beings, when neuroscience has yet to unravel the simpler sensory processes shared with other animals. We are to a large extent reliant on evidence from experimental psychology and neuropsychology, but in the following chapters I will be testing how far folk psychology can take us. Before we move on, though, we need to take a quick look at memory.

Memory

Memory is obviously central to our cognitive processes because if it were not possible to hold a concept in the mind so as to relate an associated thought to it, it would not be possible to build a cognitive synthesis. The processes of memory are not well understood but it is clear that the brain has several different memory systems[8]. Nomenclature tends to vary because we are dealing with rather soft psychological descriptions rather than any hard classification based on neurophysiology and neuroanatomy. We therefore have to make a choice in the terminology we employ, and so I have selected the three types of memory I find are most widely referred to and which offer the clearest insight into different mental processes. These are:

1.   Declarative memory
2.   Procedural memory
3.   Working memory

Declarative Memory

This is associated with conscious recall. When we remember facts or episodes in our lives we are explicitly aware of them, and for this reason it is sometimes called *explicit* memory. The hippocampus, along with closely associated regions of the cortex and limbic system, plays a central role in establishing this type of memory. This is not to say that declarative memory resides in the hippocampus, it doesn't, but the hippocampus is essential for orchestrating and laying down memory circuits in the cortex. The process for achieving long-term memory depends on the nature of the memory and so declarative memory is often subdivided into *episodic* memory (personal experience) and *semantic* memory (facts). When semantic memory is used to record facts, the hippocampal input into the neocortex must be replayed over an extended period in order to effect a 'permanent' record. Failure to do this will result in the normal process of forgetting. With episodic memory there is generally no need for such replay: we either remember an event or we do not. Sometimes, of course, we remember wrongly. The vividness with which we remember an experience is often associated with the level of emotion it generated, and so there is an element of emotional memory incorporated into most episodic memories.

Just how such memories are laid down in the brain is the subject of theory, because no one has identified a neuronal pattern associated with a particular memory. Neuroscientists have laboured for many years to identify simple memories without discovering any repeatable patterns. After extensive training of experimental animals, it seems that entirely different sets of neurons fire in response to the same stimulus and its recognition. Changes at the synaptic level in the hippocampal system have been identified when animals learn, with new synapses being formed between the axons and dendrites of connecting neurons, and existing synapses strengthened. This suggests that neuronal circuits, or maps, are in some way involved with the laying down of memories. How they get converted into your subjective recollection of your grandmother, or any similar memory, is a matter beyond the scope of present-day science.

It would be wrong to describe the brain of a newly born infant as a *tabula rasa*, because that would suggest that all neonate brains were as alike as blank slates. Clearly they are not: genetic inheritance sees to that. But, as soon as a baby starts to have experiences, neuronal maps will start to form. We may not be able to generate declarative memories at such an early age, but the memories we form later on may well depend on the structures laid down in those early maps. As we build up our episodic memories throughout our lives, new memories will depend on the neural substrate of earlier memories, so that the encoding will be different for each of us, even if we share the same experience. The picture we can build up then is of a vast network of neurons throughout the neocortex which can be activated by the hippocampus in conjunction with its associated areas in the subcortex and medial temporal cortex. Successive reactivations produce strengthening of synaptic connections, and perhaps the formation of new ones. A value will be assigned to each memory by the emotional component of limbic circuits. Until we have some idea of the number and pattern of neurons involved in specific memories, and the temporal sequence in which they fire, it has to be a matter of sheer speculation as to how the mechanism of memory works. Some neuroscientists believe there is no permanent encoding and that the neocortex relies on fluctuating dynamic patterns and an interplay between many different neuronal assemblies. These could be in the form of unrepeatable patterns exhibiting chaotic behaviour. One speculation for which there is some evidence is that episodic memory is dependent on the prefrontal cortex and semantic memory relies on medial temporal lobe regions. It is also a fairly safe assertion that linguistic memory involves the left side of the brain in most of us.

Individuals suffering from severe amnesia almost always have a failure of declarative memory, with procedural and working memory remaining largely intact. Damage may have occurred to the hippocampal system through head injury, or there may be permanent memory loss associated with prolonged and severe alcoholism (Korsakoff's syndrome) or surgical intervention affecting the hippocampus. Amnesia may be retrograde, with no memories of events prior to the trauma, or anterograde, so that no new memories are laid down over the long term and experiences are forgotten within minutes. There are many anecdotal descriptions in the literature of the devastating nature of such conditions (e.g. Oliver Sacks), and anyone familiar with Alzheimer's disease knows how distressing loss of memory can be. All these instances illustrate how important declarative memory is to the normal functioning of the human mind. Many of us have good cause to complain about the state of our memory as we get older, but as long as we can remember we have forgotten, there is no serious problem.

Procedural Memory

This involves the learning of sensory-motor skills and does not employ the hippocampal system. It is sometimes referred to under the more general heading of *non-declarative* or *implicit* memory. When we have learnt to keep our balance on a bike, remain afloat in water and tie our shoelaces, these are skills we never forget. We do not have to think about them consciously. Perhaps the most pertinent example in modern times is driving a car. Many of our actions during driving are undertaken unconsciously, to the extent that we are often unaware of large sections of a journey we have just completed, especially if it is one over which we commute regularly. Driving in town means we have to keep away from the kerb at the roadside, but we are hardly ever consciously aware of the kerb. We are, in a sense, on automatic pilot.

During learning, we have to employ consciousness as we first practise procedural skills, but as soon as we become proficient they become automatic. Subcortical structures take over the task of guiding our actions, with the basal ganglia having a central role in the process. A concert pianist playing an allegro vivace movement of a difficult sonata cannot be consciously aware of the movement of each finger, indeed there isn't time to be conscious of each note before it is played. This is similar to the situation with top class tennis players having to return a fast serve before they can be conscious of the ball reaching the net. The procedural memory required for this sort of skill is programmed into simpler and more specific neuronal structures than declarative memory and is typically unaffected by amnesia. Individuals who are unable to recall facts or recent events because of injury to the hippocampus and related nuclei still retain their basic abilities with language and their performance with many other learned tasks.

Working Memory

This encompasses the basic ability to keep track of and organise information from moment to moment. A number of investigators have identified it with the prefrontal cortex and some claim that measurements of working memory correlate strongly with performance in tasks traditionally used to measure intelligence. Bilateral damage to the frontal lobes can cause marked problems with planning and attentional control, to the extent that the prefrontal cortex has been characterised as a 'central executive' which monitors other centres in the brain and calls up selected memories. Working memory is generally unaffected in amnesia caused by hippocampal damage. Amnesiacs are able to converse normally and their performance in intelligence tests is unimpaired. This is the category of memory most closely associated with consciousness because it is absolutely essential if we are to respond to the words and actions of others. A working memory may only last for a few seconds but without it we would have difficulty in giving a good imitation of being conscious.

Analysis of working memory in primates and humans suggests that the 'central executive' idea should not be taken too literally because there appear to be multiple domains in the prefrontal cortex organised in parallel rather than any single centre. The effective operation of working memory will often depend on incorporating elements of episodic or semantic memory, so the prefrontal cortex could have a global role associated with all types of memory. The deficits that occur in individuals with damage to their frontal lobes suggests a subtle role in higher levels of cognition, and this is not at all surprising when observing the degree of development of the frontal lobes in man compared with chimpanzees, our nearest neighbours on the evolutionary scale. It will take a good deal of progress in neurobiology and cognitive psychology before a clearer picture of human brain processes can emerge, but in the meantime it may be helpful to illustrate some of the possibilities we have been considering in a not-too-serious manner.

The Minds of Frankie and Johnnie

Let me introduce you to these two characters, who are good friends. They are intelligent, honest people with no demonic characteristics, so you would be happy to know either of them. Their minds are, however, quite different because, among other things, Frankie is left-brained and Johnnie right-brained. When I speak in this manner I do not mean to imply that either of them has half their brain missing, merely that their brains have developed so that one hemisphere tends to dominate the other. Frankie is something of a linguist, speaking several foreign languages. She can write elegant prose with great facility and is a pretty competent mathematician. When involved in business activities she loves to pursue detail and some-times cannot see the wood for the trees. Johnnie always sees the big picture because he tends to develop global patterns in his mind, and he has a fine sense of structure. He has always had great difficulty with languages, especially in remembering strange vocabularies, and he isn't much of a talker, whereas Frankie can babble away nineteen-to-the-dozen. When looking at business results, Johnnie prefers to see them in the form of graphs rather than the tables that Frankie is always poring over. When they go out walking together it is always Johnnie who is the map reader. Frankie is too absorbed in the details of the walk to keep her mind on where she is going. But it isn't just the processes in their left and right hemispheres which contribute to differences in their personalities.

Frankie is the adventurous one, always seeking new, exciting experiences, whereas Johnnie is happier in familiar situations and tries to avoid over-stimulation. He likes to have a beer at lunchtime, whereas Frankie drinks coffee all day. They obviously have different neurotransmitter profiles in their subcortical systems. The likelihood is that Johnnie, being more intro-verted than Frankie, has his subcortical activity leaning more towards noradrenaline than acetylcholine (i.e. adrenergic rather than cholinergic), though, of course, both systems are active in both of them. It is a question of balance. Frankie's natural drive is much higher than Johnnie's because her thalamocortical arousal system is generally in top gear. She charges around all day and has strong views on almost every issue. Johnnie is far less emotional, with his prefrontal cortex much more clearly in charge of his limbic system, and he tends not to get passionate about things. Cool evalu-ation is his forte.

Frankie is the better golfer, with a nice, reproducible swing. Johnnie's golf swing is erratic, so it seems his basal ganglia have difficulty with his muscle memory, or is it that his frontal cortex is so active it keeps interfering with his procedural memory? Johnnie can always remember the partners he played with in his last dozen games, so there is nothing wrong with his episodic memory, but Frankie has difficulty in remembering who she last played with. Not unexpectedly though, it is always left-brained Frankie who remembers other people's names, unlike Johnnie who is excellent on faces and places, but lousy on names. There doesn't seem to be much difference in working memory with either of them, and that may account for the fact that they are well matched in general intelligence. It is not clear whether it is their differences or their similarities which make them such good friends. I hope we will meet them again later on.

Chapter 2

Observations on Mental Repertoires

Why Folk Psychology?

It sounds a bit disparaging to attach the label of folk psychology to well-recognised aspects of mind like beliefs and desires, but the fact is we are unable to characterise such attributes in terms of hard, neurophysiological descriptions. The same applies to rationality and emotion. At the simplest level, emotion and desire can be seen as motivators for action, providing the nervous activity which causes animals to act in particular ways in the interests of their own survival. A tree does not need to take action: it either survives where it stands or it dies. Presumably, this is why evolution has not found it appropriate for plants to develop nervous systems. If an organism is not going to move anywhere, it doesn't need one. All necessary nutrients for growth and reproduction are provided *in situ*, and if they aren't, too bad. Animals have a choice. They can search for nutrients, favourable environmental conditions and a sexual partner if none can be found on the spot. They could behave just like a tree, but something compels them to get up and become active, some internal state forces them to move and seek food, shelter or to reproduce. This might be characterised as the first glimmer of consciousness, where an organism becomes aware of a need to do something in its own interest. This isn't to say that the simplest animals can reflect on their own needs, as we can, but there is obviously some internal nervous activity, over and above the actual capability for movement, which causes them to take action.

Our concern, though, is not what impels primitive forms of animal life to action, but what motivates us. We know that emotions play a large part in our lives, and in later chapters we will take a harder look at what we mean by emotion, particularly those emotions we call *feelings*. For the moment I will use the two terms interchangeably. Many animals, and may be all animals except man, have to be guided largely by their emotions because the absence of language limits their ability to reason and to learn from the experience of others. It is these higher cognitive powers which equip us for rational thought and action, but it would be a mistake to think that emotion and rationality are independent of one another. The evidence suggests otherwise, as we shall see later. Philosophers over the years have examined the relationship between emotion and rationality, but since it isn't a fixed relationship it is not really a satisfactory approach to generalise for the population as a whole. We need to look at the evidence, even if that evidence is soft, and that comes down to folk psychology. Controlled studies in real life situations are virtually impossible, so we need to proceed with an assessment of the evidence available from general observation, which you can check for yourself from your own experience.

Population Thinking

Much enquiry into the mind has proceeded as though human mental processes adopt a single form. This is particularly true of the philosophical tradition relying on *essentialism* – a doctrine which concentrates on what it sees as the essential characteristics of the human condition rather than looking for the variations[1]. Although we are all built to the same basic design, we can hardly be characterised by a single prototype, especially in terms of our mental make-up. It was during the 19th century, and with Darwin in particular, that the idea of *population thinking* was introduced. This departed from essentialism in stressing that living organisms are all different from one another; each is unique, so it is inappropriate to pin down descriptions to a single, inflexible formula. Modern science is concerned with measurement and description, and it makes no presupposition about any homogeneity in a population. Where there are similarities in structure or function, these are identified, but so are the variations that occur naturally. Much philosophy still proceeds on the basis of essentialism because by its very nature it is concerned with theorising about prototypical features of mankind and it does not examine evidence from population studies. In considering the mind, there is, unfortunately, very little hard population evidence to draw on, and so we have to contend with a lot of theory and many anecdotal accounts.

In the first paragraph of the *Introduction* I mentioned the profound impression that my own experience had made on me when observing the different ways people's minds worked. The community in which I spent my business career was an intelligent one, as might be expected in a technologically based sector of industry. Integrity and civilised values were a defining characteristic, and at no time did I come across utterly unreasonable behaviour. My own company had a culture to which an outside observer might have attributed a degree of greyness, but that would be rather like saying all Japanese look alike. Within that outwardly monochrome culture there was a rich variety of ideas and views, so that to the last days of my career I was taken by surprise by unexpected aspects of individual personalities, often of people I had known for many years. In many ways we cruise across the surface of each other's outward personalities with little idea about what may be going on in the submerged depths of the inner mind. Although we have all developed our own *theory of mind* which helps us to gauge what others might be thinking, we often fall back on our own mental processes as a template for judging the responses of others. In psychological jargon this has been described as *off-line simulation:* running through in your own mind what you might think in someone else's situation. In practice, I guess most of us use a combination of the two approaches.

Inevitably, the observations I have made of other people during the course of my working life are confined to a restricted sample of the population. I have had no first-hand experience, worth speaking of, of criminally or violently inclined individuals, of people who live on an academic or artistic plane, of the socially deprived, of the landed gentry, or of a myriad other sectors. Like most people, I have lived my life within a community which has had only limited areas of intersection with other circles of society. Whether we are philosophers, scientists, politicians or industrialists, our outlook tends to be coloured by the sector in which we spend the greater part of our active lives. In my own case I have lived in Japan and the United States, and I spent a lot of time in continental Western Europe, so I can claim to have a fairly broad exposure to different cultures. My activities were largely confined to the industrial and medical communities, though on an international scale. That does not make me an expert on people, but it has given me an opportunity to observe a broad selection of personalities and to appreciate how great is the variety even within a restricted population.

Many psychological tests have been carried out on a population basis, measuring aspects of personality or intelligence. I have seen these used in an interesting way by psychologist Meredith Belbin for selecting people to compete in a business game. The results of the tests allowed him to predict, with an impressive degree of success, which team would win and which wouldn't. He could forecast how the team members were likely to interact and how effective the emergent-algorithm of the team would be. But this tells us very little about how individual brains work, and why they work that way. On the whole, psychological testing has given us surprisingly little insight into the mind because it cannot measure what is going on inside people's heads. Why is Ramsbotham sullen and awkward, disrupting the team's progress, despite his high intelligence? What is it that makes the dullards in Team B co-operate so effectively and achieve such impressive results? If we could trace the circuitry of the billions of neurons in each brain it wouldn't tell us much about the whole, even if we could manage the mathematics involved, because the emergent properties of a self-organising system like the brain cannot be predicted from an examination of the individual components. The constituent parts are so interdependent they lose their character if separated from the whole. We have to examine the problem at another level, and a good place to start is with the areas of our central nervous system known to be involved in our emotional make-up.

The Head or the Heart?

No one with any anatomical knowledge at all now believes that the heart has anything to do with our emotions in a strict functional sense. Yet it remains a useful symbol of our emotional reaction to experience. For this to happen on such a universal scale it must mean that the nervous control of the heart produces important signals to many people about their emotional state. So powerful is its influence that it can often be the main determinant of action in personal life and in cementing relationships. If someone is described as 'having no heart' it is likely they are going to run into difficulties in establishing the warm relationships that add so much to the joyful side of life. But there is a converse side. When we are under stress or frightened we may become aware of our racing heart. This can be accompanied by a number of other unpleasant somatic (body) symptoms, such as a sinking feeling in our abdomen, muscle tremor, clammy skin, dry mouth and breathlessness. You may even be able to precipitate a hint of one of these symptoms by recalling an event or circumstance that you find unpalatable. Conscious thoughts can trigger the emotional centres of the subcortex and their control of the autonomic nervous system. This provides a feedback system from the body which has a lot to do with determining how we feel. It can and does act fast, so we often find ourselves responding emotionally before we have really had time to sort out our ideas.

It might be thought that emotional responses require only a simple reflex action on the part of the nervous system, rather like drawing our hand away form a hot stove. But that is far from the reality, because emotions are associated with images in the mind and these in themselves involve vast numbers of neurons. This can be illustrated by taking the example of someone who has a particular aversion, say to spiders; something more than a simple dislike but less than a phobia. A sudden image of a spider in the mind, whether from direct perception or visual recall from memory will trigger circuits in the cerebral cortex involving millions of neurons. Activated zones in the sensory cortex will link up with the evaluative centres in the frontal cortex and instruct subcortical structures how to react. It is the subcortex which controls the emotional response. The signal that eventually reaches the hypothalamus and determines whether it activates the autonomic nervous system will probably depend on years of training of neuronal networks in the higher centres. A young child seeing a spider for the first time has no particular attitude, no more than it does in seeing a chair for the first time. But the emotional response of the mother or other close family members will begin to train the response of the child's neuronal networks. Creepy, crawliness is an idea which most of us find un-pleasant, but there are those in whom it causes no reaction at all. Spiders, at least in temperate climates, are not harmful, so why do we develop this aversion? Cultural training is the likely explanation.

Perhaps the dominant 'spider sense' is touch. How many of us will happily pick up a spider or let one crawl across our skin? It is difficult to produce a rational reason for our attitude. In the end, it doesn't matter whether we pick up spiders or not, so we are content to remain with our irrationality. The important point is that we should be able to acknowledge we are being irrational in having a spider aversion. There are plenty of other examples in every-day life of emotional reactions to things we see and hear. Newspapers and television play on this fact because they know it is what sells their product. We like to have our indignation stirred or our sympathy engaged, without any real insight into the veridicality of the story being portrayed. The media appeals to the romantic in all of us by addressing the heart rather than the head. We are governed, much of the time, by the way our conscious thoughts link into our limbic system, and the way this hedonic centre of the brain drives our autonomic nervous system and pro-duces feedback into conscious awareness. Thinking emotionally is fast and requires little effort. In our personal lives it often gives us as good a result as thinking and reasoning in a rational manner, which takes time and requires considerable conscious effort. But when it comes to the wider scene, inappropriate emotion and poor understanding of risk and probability can lead us badly astray, as the UK government found with its handling of the BSE crisis.

Yet, not many of us are totally led by our emotions. We often jump to conclusions as individuals, but on reflection and interaction with other people we modify our views as new facts and interpretations become avail-able. We give the algorithm of rational thought time to emerge. There is no question that it takes time to think rationally because the speed at which we can assess all the arguments is several orders of magnitude slower than it takes for our feelings to come flooding to the surface. But the final result of any rational deliberation is likely to be a feeling which will determine the decision we make. There are not many instances in life where we can be absolutely certain of the right course of action through logical analysis, so we have to make our decisions on the balance of probabilities, even if we do not realise that is where our feelings are leading us.

Where Does Rationality Fit in?

We could have a long philosophical debate on possible definitions for rationality, but the working definition I would like to use for the purpose of my examination is *'the assignment of probability to belief in calculating outcomes or making judgements'*. This will be regarded by many as only one sense of rationality, but I will make the claim that it is the sense most appropriate for considering every-day activities. It means that every time we have a conviction we have to examine the evidence and ask ourselves what the chances are of it being valid. The more complex and uncertain a situation the greater the need to exercise judgement. The task may seem daunting in situations where we are confronted by conflicting views, say, caught between two experts who disagree with one another; something which happens with monotonous regularity in debates about the mind and consciousness. We should not worry too much about dissension in the philosophical camp because philosophers enjoy debates about logical possibilities centred on contradictory metaphysical speculations not instantiated in the real world. Many are not concerned with assessing evidence and prefer *a priori* arguments, though it has to be said there is a nucleus of philosophers of mind steeped in neuroscience and cognitive psychology who do weigh the evidence.

Even in the scientific world there are often conflicting theories, and if anything is supposed to be rational it's science. Evidence for a particular theory may be inconclusive, but its proponents will often express total con-viction about their position. This may facilitate the dialectic and iterative process which allows advance to take place, but it is to be hoped that any advocacy for a particular position is tempered by an acknowledgement of the possibility that the proponents may have backed the wrong horse. This can lead to difficult emotional positions when a lifetime of work is at stake, but this is the gamble scientists take. If there is disagreement about matters of fact someone will be proved wrong in the long haul, and it will be the emergent-algorithm of scientific progress that sorts it out. In the field of experimental psychology the behaviourists held sway for most of the first half of this century, and now their views are more or less dismissed. The same applies to much of the theorising of Freud and his psychoanalytical disciples.

If we move to more commonly observed areas of daily life it is easier to see where rationality and irrationality come into play. Take the instance of politicians making statements about their chances of being re-elected. Most people would accept that to concede the possibility of defeat before an election would not be very smart. The rational stance is that there is always a chance of defeat, but conventions do not allow politicians to admit the fact without damaging their chances, so we allow the charade without drawing conclusions as to the state of their mind. Nevertheless, we hope that our potential leaders of the future have a better grasp of the realities than they are allowed to say. Irrational opinions can often arise because of 'availability error' – the tendency to draw conclusions on inadequate evidence[2]. We have all listened to or participated in conversations where the debaters hold forth on a subject of national importance – perhaps the intellectual competence of the Prime Minister. Whatever the state of the Prime Minister's mind may be, we can be sure that the discussants do not have sufficient information to make a valid judgement about its capacities – the information is not 'available'. They are probably basing their opinions on comments made in a tabloid newspaper or on a television report, without making any allowance for lack of objectivity or sheer prejudice on the part of the reporting medium. We all do it, and it can be fun, but how many people are consciously aware they are being irrational?

More serious instances of availability error can be observed in organisations considering issues of greater import, issues that have practical consequences. Many a boardroom discussion in the nations' great companies exhibits this phenomenon when directors express views about an investment project or a subsidiary's performance, based on a very limited amount of evidence. Of course, directors have to take a stance on the facts available to them, but how many of them consciously register the flimsiness of the evidence on which their opinion is based, or that the probability of their view being justified is quite low? Of course, in making this observation about boardroom discussions I can myself be accused of 'availability error', because I have limited direct evidence of what goes on in such meetings, but it is possible for observers to note the incidence of bad decisions that reach the public domain and to draw the inference alongside their own first-hand experience.

One of the problems in achieving ideal levels of rationality is that we all look at the world from a skewed perspective – that of self. Our own cause is more important to us than any other, and our own opinion consequently more highly rated. Self-belief may be crucial for prosperous survival, but it does not provide the best basis for rational deliberation when all arguments have to be weighed evenly. On the other hand, if we could see all our own

faults and weaknesses as starkly as other people see them we might hesitate
in every action, and that would not do our cause much good in a competitive world. High self-esteem is an important ingredient in success, and my
experience is that people generally have it in abundance. I have never come
across an unequivocal example of low self-esteem, though some people are
more realistic about their abilities than others. The best way to get an objective fix on ability levels is to tap the consensus view in the organisation
of which the individual is a member. This provides the emergent-algorithm
of the collective mind, which will give the fairest judgement. Performance
will have been assessed from many different angles over a period of time
with the emergence of a discernible and reliable pattern of opinions about
individuals. I have never known it let me down.

Belief is central to the issue of rationality, and that is why assessment of
the basis of people's convictions and their validity is fundamental to its
practical application. When confronted by an issue we have to ask, 'What is
the strength of the evidence and what is the balance of probabilities?' I will
leave a more detailed examination of belief until the next chapter, but it is
worthwhile at this stage making a distinction between belief and faith. All
belief is buttressed by emotion because in the end our feelings determine
what we believe, and the strength with which we believe it. But my use of
belief will be reserved for describing an attitude of mind directed towards
those issues which are, in principle, open to resolution at some stage.
Where such resolution is not possible and belief becomes so deeply
imbedded in the emotional structure of the mind that it takes on the mantle
of certainty in the face of a multiplicity of conflicting views, I will con-
sign to the realms of faith. Religious faith falls into this category. It is
important in many people's lives and I would like to leave it outside the
bounds of my discussion of belief and rationality, because it will only
confuse arguments related to judgements about the world we experience
from day to day.

Statistics and the Mind

Rationality, even in a working or informal sense, is something more than
simply sorting out our beliefs, though, because it requires they are preceded
by a process of reasoning and subjected to a degree of cognitive evaluation.
The conscious effort required can be demanding and may result in mental
strain if carried on for too long without some form of diversion. Perhaps
that's why we so often fail to analyse our beliefs in any great depth. To help
us move forward in considering the neuronal processes involved, I am

going to return to our three blocks of the brain as a useful schematic framework. You will recall that the *subcortex* centres on the thalamus, basal ganglia and limbic system, coupled with the reticular formation. We can regard this as the power source and emotional centre of the brain, which is also in charge of our autonomic nervous system. The *sensory cortex* provides our sensory processing areas, which also allows us to communicate with others. It is located in the occipital, parietal and temporal areas of the cerebral hemispheres, with language on the left side and the capacity to structure spatial concepts, including those of our body, on the right. Our awareness of the world around us is processed in the sensory cortex. It is interesting that virtually all our sensory inputs get to this area via the subcortex. This indicates the possibility of our sensations being coloured by emotional overtones because of the complex interlinking circuits, and experience suggests this should not come as any surprise. The *frontal cortex* is the most highly evolved part of the human brain. It is here we plan our lives and rationalise the world around us, including developing an awareness of ourselves. The frontal cortex receives its inputs via the sensory cortex and subcortex, so there is no way it can escape the value charged overtones resident in these other centres. It is unlikely that any centre can work in isolation, so we can visualise the situation as a number of interacting circuits involving vast numbers of neurons connecting the three blocks. We can utilise this as a general scheme of things, at the same time appreciating that there is very little hard evidence on the circuits that are in operation and that, in any case, they will show considerable variation from one individual to another, including the observable characteristics they generate. The balance between the different centres and the extent to which neuronal maps have been developed will produce a wide diversity of minds within the population. We can get some idea of this variation by borrowing a statistical concept used in population studies – *frequency distribution* and the bell-shaped curve.

If we plot the height of everyone in a particular population we will get a bell-shaped curve (Figure 2), with the mean height of the population corresponding to the apex of the curve. The majority of the population lies within a certain deviation from that mean. Exceptional tallness or exceptional smallness lie at the extremes of the curve and involve small numbers of people. The flatter the shape of the curve the wider the variation in the distribution of the characteristic. Most of us are familiar with the plotting of the results of I.Q. tests in this way, and it would be difficult to find a more accessible explanation of this subject than that given in Appendix 1 of *The Bell Curve* by Herrnstein and Murray[3], which is a study of intelligence and class structure. Measuring height distributions is not controversial, but measuring I.Q. distributions has proved to be so. With rationality we find it difficult enough to define it, let alone measure it, so we would certainly be entering a minefield in trying to carry out any practical study of the characteristic. But supposing we could develop an index, we would expect to find a bell-shaped distribution ranging from low to high with the great majority of the population around the mean.

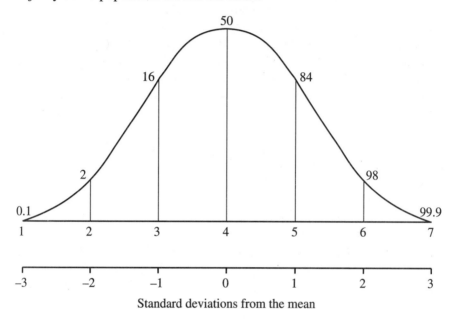

Figure 2 *The bell-shaped distribution curve*

Let's imagine, for the moment, that we are able to construct a measure that would give us an index of rationality on a scale of 1 to 7 and that we are allowed to apply the conventions of the statistical method to aid our own thinking. The reason for choosing the range 1 to 7 is because it is convenient for representing the population in terms of standard deviations from the mean (Figure 2). Anyone scoring 4 is plumb in the centre of the population distribution. 68% of the population falls between 3 and 5, 96% between 2 and 6, and 99.7% between 1 and 7. The numbers around the top of the bell curve are percentiles, when thinking in terms of 'above' and 'below' the mean. If we were considering height, the tallest 2% would score 6 or above, i.e. would be 98th percentile, and the smallest 2% would score 2 or below, i.e. would be 2nd percentile. If we are now considering a scale of rationality, with '1' representing the most irrational members of society, and anything above '6' the top 2% of high scorers on rationality, where would you be most like to fall on this scale? My guess is that nearly all readers would plump for being as rational as possible, because almost everyone, in my experience, likes to think of themselves in this way. To call someone irrational is to be thought of as flinging an insult at them. If we were now to stretch our imagination a little further we could perhaps visualise a being whose frontal lobes had developed to such an extent that they were able to totally suppress the emotional centres of the brain. Perhaps you are now not so sure you want to be totally rational if it means being a colourless automaton. Fortunately, there is not much chance of that for any of us, but if we have sufficient self-insight we should be able to make a reasonable appraisal of our actions and attitudes and their rationality quotient.

To be totally rational we would need brains that could assess all the evidence, calculate all the probabilities for possible outcomes and apply the principles of deductive logic. This is hardly a practical option, so we have to take an intuitive short cut and follow the path we *believe* to be right. The amount of evidence brought to bear and analysed will vary greatly, as will the extent to which emotional circuits are activated. Consequently, the population becomes divided into many different camps on every conceivable issue, each believing it has the best answer, sometimes bolstered by the strongest of emotions. Why do we believe what we do with such fervour, when we know our particular belief is diametrically opposed to someone else's? It can hardly be due to rationality. The evidence on which the belief is based is generally inconclusive, so a purely rational stance would recognise that fact and assign only a probability to the chance of our belief being the correct one. Not many people behave in that way, and those who do tend to get trampled in the crush. It seems evolution of our society into a more calmly reflective one is up against a serious obstacle. Rational reflection has an air of passivity about it, levels of social influence often being determined by the energising centres in the subcortex – the centres that generate all the emotion. Emotion is the fuel which provides the motive power. Once again we can see great differences between individuals in the levels of drive and energy they possess, ranging from the great achievers of this world, to those who might be described as 'inactive'. Look around you and it will not be difficult to allot a score on 'drive' to the people you know on a scale of 1 to 7, and if your circle of acquaintances is large enough you should be able to plot the outlines of a bell-shaped distribution curve. Is there a correlation between those who score highly on rationality and those who score highly on emotional energy? I do not suppose the study has been done, and my bet would be that there is a very low correlation. Why should we expect one? We do not expect the middle distance runner to be a weight lifter. Of course, there will be some who benefit from a large helping of both attributes, because there is no reason to believe they are mutually exclusive, but if the correlation is low it probably means that rationality often gets steamrollered by emotional aggression. You might agree that this seems to correspond with experience.

Processing Perceptions

In our simplified scheme of things we must not forget the sensory cortex, where the awareness of the world around us and an image of our own bodily orientation resides. But to be aware of something we have to pay attention; observation requires an object. How we decide what to observe is still shrouded in mystery. Clearly, if something attracts our attention in a dramatic way, like being stung by a bee or seeing a traffic accident, there is a straightforward case of cause and effect, but if we are sitting in a quiet room, leafing through a magazine, it is not so easy to be sure. Some things stand out as being emotionally triggered, such as if there is a sexually explicit image, because such reactions are pretty universal. The advertising agencies are well aware of the power of the hypothalamus, even if they don't know what it is. If we push this a little further we can make a case for much perception and attention being triggered by areas of interest stored in our memories, and these will vary from person to person. Interest may be associated with high-performance cars, *cordon bleu* food, hi-fi or the latest *haute couture* fashions, depending on the level of emotional arousal they stimulate.

For our purposes we can consider the sensory cortex as the repository of sensory images. When it registers a particular scene it will be selective about which elements it gives emphasis to and how it interprets them, depending on how complex the stimulus happens to be. Simple cognitive tests throw only limited light on what happens in the real world. If we are asked to describe a chair standing in the corner of a room it is likely that descriptions provided by different persons will show a high degree of correlation, to such an extent that it might be thought there is an 'objective' perception of the chair. But that is only because the perception in this instance is so straightforward it is not disrupted by a host of other neuronal circuits pre-established in the brain. If we consider an experience at the other end of the complexity spectrum, say a Wagner opera, it will soon become obvious that the situation is quite different. For a start it depends on our point of observation: are we the bass singing Wotan, a member of the orchestra, or a member of the audience? If in the audience, are we a critic

writing a review of the performance, a Wagner lover seeing a live performance for the first time, or a bored member of the family who has been
dragged along? What level of concentration can we maintain, how deep is
our knowledge of the music, and can we understand German? The number
of variables from individual to individual is immense, and yet, in the end a
consensus will emerge as to whether it was a five-star performance or only
a two-star performance. That is a statistical outcome, with the views of any
one person being of very limited value, except to themselves. This is where
rational assessment enters the equation: the ability to make a fair assessment of the informed population view, even though there is less than full
empathy for Wagner. For Wagner we can substitute a rock concert, an
Islamic chant, a Japanese Noh play, or an American football game.

Perception is influenced by background, by the years we have spent
learning to understand the context of what we hear and see, and by the
conventions we have absorbed. Where is all this stored? Obviously in our
memories, but at the same time there must be an emotional value attributed
to a memory for us to decide how we respond to it: with a degree of
pleasurable satisfaction, with indifference or with displeasure. For most of
us a chair is a chair, and the image of one does not evoke any particular,
affective overtones. That is why we can all readily agree it is a chair. But if
we are asked for our reaction to the status of a political figure and their
activities, it is unlikely such universal agreement will be achieved. To some
the politician may represent an idol, to others they may represent a hate
figure. So here we have an interaction between the perceived image in front
of us, our earlier memories of it and the emotions they engender, and our
conscious assessment of the present situation. This last ingredient is where
the frontal cortex plays an essential role, because it is necessary to form and
sustain our judgement on how the politician's record rates against the track
record of others, and what this suggests their future performance may be.
Whether the politician gets elected or not depends on the aggregated decision of a multitude of individuals: it is a population outcome, even though
it may be achieved on the basis of a sparse number of hard facts.

Even attempting the limited analysis we have undertaken in our simplified framework we can see that we are faced with a situation of daunting
complexity. Our perceptions located in the sensory cortex, which in themselves require immense powers of computation, are filtered through a
subjective haze determined by the background and conventions we have
absorbed into our memories and the responses they elicit from the emotional centres in the subcortex. These are then integrated with our powers of
reflection and evaluation in the frontal cortex, so that we produce a
conscious judgement. If this judgement remains locked inside our own ego,

with very little regard being paid to contradictory views that others may hold, then it is likely we will end up with beliefs that have foundations less solid than they otherwise might be. Think of all the people who are totally sure they are right, who fundamentally disagree with you! Rationality could help human culture step outside this subjective *impasse*.

Romantics and Realists

Is it possible to make any assessment of the degree of rationality individuals apply to their thinking? Pretty clearly, we are not able to do it on any agreed scientific basis. Simply look at the furore that the time-tested and relatively straightforward measurement of cognitive ability (I.Q.) produces and we could see what deep water we would be getting into. However, each of us is able to play our own game, unbeknown to anyone else, that enables us to make our own assessment of someone's rationality rating. To do this we need to employ the bell shaped curve and the ranking of 1 to 7 that we used earlier. Instead of plotting from *irrational* at one end to *rational* at the other, we need to find a less emotive scheme. I am going to suggest we employ the terms *romantic* and *realist*, where romantic designates a tendency to be dominated by ones own inner thoughts and ideas, and realist indicates a hard-nosed capacity to assess the external world and a sensitivity to its reactions. In order to demonstrate there is no pejorative intent I am going to allocate a ranking of 1 to the highest score on realism at one end of the scale, and 7 to romanticism at the other end. In this case we are not talking about above and below the mean, but either side of the mean. (At this point we must muffle the cries of outrage from purist statisticians!) Someone with an even balance of romanticism and realism will score near the mean, i.e. 4. 68% of the population will fall between 3 and 5, and 96% of us will fall between 2 and 6. All of this, of course, takes place only in our mind's eye.

Before you start rating your friends and acquaintances, let alone yourself, you might like a trial run by thinking of some historical figures. Let's take Hitler, Stalin, Roosevelt and Churchill. We have to ignore all their other attributes but the one we are considering. Of course, we do not really know enough about them to be absolutely confident about our judgements, so we will have to award a provisional mark on what we do know. As an aside, before I stick my neck out, I recall that Bernard Levin, in one of his *Times* articles, once had the temerity (though he blamed it on a friend) to construct a series of teams from composers, starting with the *Superstars*. This top team included obvious names like Mozart, Beethoven and Wagner, but when it came to the 9th, 10th and 11th members of the team the choices became much more contentious. We have to rank our historical characters with the same sort of intrepid recklessness. Who, in our quartet, would score highest on romanticism? Probably not much disagreement on this one in choosing Hitler because he was 'romantic' to the point of being deluded. What about realism? Churchill was certainly realistic about Hitler and Stalin was realistic about how to maintain power in a totalitarian state, but both tended to get carried away by their own egos, Churchill by his imagination and Stalin by his paranoia: though Stalin, as he once confided to Anthony Eden, 'knew when to stop', unlike Hitler. Would Churchill have taken his stance in 1940 if he had had a true appreciation of the odds? The mystery man is Franklin Roosevelt, and this is probably the clue to him being the greatest realist, for such people rarely declare themselves openly. Roosevelt, reportedly, used to set one part of his administration against another to see who would come out on top. A true pragmatist. He was also cautiously clever in the way he gradually edged the United States into the Second World War in a decisive historical step. True, towards the end of his Presidency, when he was very ill, he became overconfident in his powers of personal influence and was manipulated by Stalin, but then none of us presents a clean profile. Churchill is one of history's great leaders and, if his romanticism coincided with the times, this takes nothing away from his colossal talents. Historically, it could be argued, most great leaders have been romantics, but what about the future in our technological age? My own 'realist' to 'romantic' order would be Roosevelt, Stalin, Churchill, Hitler.

This may sound rather outrageous, based on such flimsy evidence, but in making judgements about people in real life we generally confine them to our own mental space. In any case, we are not in a position to administer the equivalent of a Personality Factor Inventory, where a whole series of questions can be asked before determining an individual's score. Anyone familiar with psychometric tests knows they can be used to assess whether a person is tough minded or tender minded, sociable or unsociable, anxious or calm, and where they stand on a whole series of other personality measures. In judging whether someone's cognitive processes are similar to our own or not we obviously have to rely on external clues and, as with personality assessment, it should be possible to devise a whole series of categories by which to evaluate mental constructs. This, however, is likely to have limited value in practical situations. As already mentioned, I have seen personality tests used very effectively in selecting teams to compete in a situation where the experimenter has been given a free hand, but my experience suggests that such tests are hardly practicable in a working organisation where everyone has a particular job to do and teams have to be formed on the basis of expertise rather than personality factors. In such situations there is likely to be a random spectrum of mental repertoires within a particular group, and what you need to gauge is, how probable is it that your colleagues' appreciation of the external facts synchronise with your own?

A Structural Axis

Before we can proceed further, though, we should consider another aspect of the thinking process associated with rationality, where it might be useful to regard it as a matter of right brain versus left brain dominance. Have you noticed how some people string thoughts together in an order which makes little sense to you? In fact you may know someone who can recount anecdote after anecdote in an impressively articulate manner but who has difficulty in ending up with coherent, structured concepts. It is certainly a differentiation that has impressed itself on me, and once again using our bell-shaped distribution curve I find it useful to have a mental plot on an axis of *structural* at one end to *anecdotal* at the other. Not only is it a classification apparent in conversation, but it also appears clearly in written texts. Perhaps the supreme structuralist was Charles Darwin, whose great masterpiece *The Origin of Species* is not only a delight to read but also gives you a sense throughout that the big picture he is putting together is totally thought through. Of course, we have the benefit of the historical validation of his views, but reading *The Origin of Species* makes it evident why Darwin made the impact he did on evolutionary theory. At the other end of the spectrum, every time I read anything about Freud I am struck by the totally anecdotal nature of his writings and, although he certainly made an impact, he is quite peripheral to the modern, scientific study of the mind. I do not know where you would stand on the '1' to '7' spectrum, but the chances are you fall within one standard deviation of my hypothetical mean and have a pretty even balance of anecdotal and structural thinking.

I do not want to push these rationality criteria of *realist/romantic* and *structural/anecdotal* too far; they are simply crude tools for getting a grasp of whether someone else's thought processes match your own or not. If you don't like these categories I would invite you to design your own, but at least those I am proposing do have the merit of providing observable clues, even though scoring of them may be subject to wild degrees of error. Whatever categorisations we use there is a crucially related aspect of mental processing which does not provide any obvious external clues about what is going on. This involves the facility with which we can employ our memories. There are obviously vast differences in our memories and the way we can retrieve them, and to confine examination of memory to a single, essentialist approach seems unlikely to be very productive. Some people have strong semantic memories where they are able to remember facts and names with great facility, others rely on their episodic memories and can recount details in their personal histories in great detail. Some memories are essentially verbal, others are visual, and there are probably many variants in between. Whatever guise they take they are a vital component of our cognitive processes, and if there is a memory deficit for any reason the handicap soon becomes all too apparent. This ability to utilise memory is essential for the formation of our beliefs and for calculating their importance in the formulation of our rational processes.

Variables of Mind

For most of the time that we are in a state of wakefulness our senses dominate our conscious awareness and most of us seek gratification from external stimuli wherever possible, whether from interaction with friends and colleagues, from physical activity, or from the more passive absorption of images from visual or auditory media. These sensations are often accompanied by a subconscious sense of bodily orientation and the movement of our limbs (proprioception). If we are on a country walk we rarely think about the act of walking or the way we swing our arms if our muscles and joints are in good working order, but we are conscious of the terrain and the scenery, and the country sounds or the chatter from a companion. This is what makes the walk interesting. The *sensations* we become aware of are likely to stimulate *memories* and some kind of *emotional response*. At its most primitive, Gerald Edelman describes this as the 'remembered present', since the evidence suggests that other species react in a similar way to human beings. The place in which they find themselves is familiar or unfamiliar, it threatens danger or offers safety, it is somewhere where there is a likelihood of gaining reward (such as food or shelter) or there is not. But, as human beings, we then move on to a different mental level because our possession of *language* enables us to benefit from a broader cultural inheritance than just our own individual experience. We start to analyse our situation and formulate our plans according to our background of knowledge and our assessment of what is likely to bring satisfaction. For that we require processes which we can group under the broad heading of *rationality*.

In the next chapter I examine some of the elements of folk psychology in greater depth and I will make use of this limited selection of variables of mind – sensations, memory, emotion, language, rationality – to see if they will give us a better fix on a broad range of mental repertoires involved in explanations of behaviour.

Chapter 3

A Deeper Excursion into Folk Psychology

Self-interest and Self-awareness

Anyone working in a large organisation is forced to become an amateur psychologist from time to time as they try to interpret the motives and intentions of colleagues. Obviously, if you are trying to read another person's mind it is very important to know if what they are saying is what they really think, and sometimes it needs a bit of detective work to find out. It is easy for the most astute of us to be deceived, especially if we are honest and straightforward, because we automatically project our own attributes on to the other person. We believe what they say. But the other person may be inherently devious and deliberately set out to give us the wrong impression, for their own purposes. Once again, if we employ our frequency distribution model of the population, we can identify a complete spectrum of behavioural integrity, from totally honest (in the way that George Washington was supposed to be) to constitutionally devious, with most of us having a mixture of these attributes. What aspects of the brain are at work here? Animal studies suggest that the neocortex is intimately involved because deliberately deceptive behaviour is only observed in primates, and the frequency with which tactical deception is reported for different species of monkeys and apes correlates well with the relative sizes of their neocortices and the complexity of their social behaviour. There is no evidence that any animal species, other than monkey and ape, can formulate behaviour with intent to deceive[1].

The ability to read social situations and to influence them in a direction of self-interest would seem to require a lot of computing power, and evolution has made ample provision for it in the case of human beings. If short-term self-interest were the sole motivating force, it might suggest that the cleverest deceiver had a winning strategy, but fortunately there are countervailing forces in any stable social group because other members of the community are likely to take appropriate anti-cheating action. Against the possible success of deception, our brains have to calculate probable outcomes for our long-term interests within the community, and that requires us to make some assessment of how others see us – to be self-aware. There is a long-standing theoretical conundrum, exemplified as the

Prisoner's Dilemma, where achieving the best outcome for yourself depends on predicting correctly what another person is going to do. It turns out that, if the game is repeated numerous times, one of the best strategies is the simplest[2]. You behave co-operatively on the first occasion and subsequently do as your opponent did on the previous occasion – a 'tit-for-tat' strategy. Cheating can pay once, but if you are going to stick around you will almost certainly receive a dose of your own medicine in the future. In such a situation learning takes place rapidly and both parties find it best to co-operate.

Self-awareness can be considered as one of the highest products of human evolution, one step ahead of consciousness itself. As far as we can tell, other species have only rudimentary self-awareness or perhaps none at all. Although there is evidence that chimpanzees can recognise their own image in a mirror, there is no convincing evidence that dogs can. When we get to the stage of worrying about our own mortality and what happens to us after death, we are in a class of our own. Self-interest is something rather different since it is related to self-preservation and is programmed into our emotional system. The 'fight or flight' characteristic is one shared with many animals, as is the urge to hunt for food. Just as well, otherwise survival would be in jeopardy. The subcortex, and particularly the hypothalamus with its control of the sympathetic nervous system, determines the extent to which adrenaline and noradrenaline flood into our muscular and visceral system. If we are threatened or angered our heart rate increases dramatically because of sympathetic stimulation and our attention becomes entirely focussed on the issue at hand. When we have calmed down a bit we can review the situation we found ourselves in and analyse our actions. This is where self-awareness and the application of rationality come in.

It may be helpful to consider a practical example where emotional override can determine our behaviour and rational calculation goes out of the window for a time. If I am stranded at the wrong terminal in a big international airport and I have 30 minutes to catch my flight I am likely to take desperate measures to commandeer a taxi, even if it means making exaggerated promises about the level of payment. I am unlikely to meet the taxi driver again and the sense of panic that overwhelms me obliterates considerations of honouring my word when I know I have only a certain amount of local currency left in my pocket. I give the driver what I have and dash for the plane. The adrenaline is pumping, I can't think clearly, I am in a 'fight or flight' mode. Depending on your own disposition, this example may seem apt or inapt, but it doesn't need much imagination to develop a bespoke scenario for any individual where they would lose their cool and behave in a less than straightforwardly honourable manner. If anything, the incidence of such behaviour seems to be increasing, as tales of impetuous, anti-social actions mushroom in the media. Road rage is an example. None of us is immune from the effects of the emotional pressure of the moment. On quiet reflection, though, we should be able to examine our behaviour in a rational manner and recognise it as being less than admirable. Some minds seem to have difficulty in achieving this. There will be cases where individuals cannot remember exactly what they promised, or they may have processed images that appear to justify their action, or they simply will not be able to recognise how badly they have behaved. Rationality will have failed because there is a less than objective evaluation of self.

Self-interest is a state that is always with us because it is programmed into our genetic make-up by the requirements of evolution ('the selfish gene'). With some people it will manifest itself all the time, and with others it will only become apparent when their vital interests are at stake. Self-awareness enables us to get a degree of insight into aspects of our self-interest, and to analyse the forces at play. It is highly probable that our frontal lobes are central to this process but they have to operate within the ambit of folk psychological elements that are fundamental to determining our behaviour and which have a significant emotional component – our beliefs and our desires.

Belief

Belief can be analysed from a philosophical or a psychological viewpoint but it would be very difficult at this stage of our knowledge to make a neuroscientific statement about the matter. Insufficient is known about neuronal structures involved in belief, and since most neuroscientific investigations are carried out in experimental animals, it is hard to see how progress is going to be made with research programmes at this level. Philosophers will comment on the nature of a proposition that is believed and they will class the resultant belief as a *propositional attitude*. Such an analysis gets involved in the subtleties of language and how words and sentences can be interpreted. Psychologists will examine the circumstances under which people believe certain things, such as the effect from influence of peer groups. Group situations enhance the confidence with which individuals hold their beliefs, and under certain conditions they can persuade people to adopt beliefs which are contrary to their own instincts. There is psychological pressure to conform and avoid what has been called *cognitive dissonance*. We look for reassurance in our beliefs, and that usually comes from other people in what they say or what they write. For our purpose we need to consider belief at the level we meet it in every-day situations and to see if there is any way we can relate what is going on in the mind to the way the brain operates.

It seems clear that belief encompasses a whole spectrum of mental states. We can believe something on a balance of probabilities or we can believe something with total conviction. Belief, in some instances, can take on the mantle of certainty, as in the case of much religious belief, and in other instances it can be merely the expression of a probable outcome, like which racing driver will win the Grand Prix or which golfer the Masters. In the latter cases a degree of rational calculation must be brought to bear because the judgement is generally based on recent evidence. In the case of religious belief there is a strong emotional factor often founded on cultural upbringing and coupled with subtle effects of language and interactions with other believers. You will recall I am reserving this type of belief for the realm of faith and leaving it outside our considerations.

Cultural influences also have some impact on political beliefs, but these have to be balanced against perceived outcomes and calculated self-interest. Cultural influences often seem unpredictable in that young adults quite frequently take radically different stances to their parents or other early guiding influences. The degree to which rationality is brought to bear in holding a political belief is difficult to discern because, in a democracy, political persuasions tend to divide into opposing camps, each believing it has the true solution to social and economic issues. Since they take distinctly different idealistic positions, which the evidence suggests often lead them down the wrong track in reaching their prescribed utopia, it is a source of wonder that they stick so rigidly to their dogmas. Here, group influences can come to bear. Competitive and reinforcement elements enter into the equation, preventing one camp poaching from the other's domain and still preserving credibility. No doubt totalitarian regimes adopting a Marxist creed thought they had the answer to this dilemma but, unfortunately for them, their economic philosophy proved to be flawed.

We can be fairly confident that belief enters into our mental processes as a primary influence when we are confronted with issues that are so complex or so uncertain there are no clear answers. If we *know* something it should be possible to demonstrate that it is true, and if this is not possible we have to resort to belief as a sub-optimal strategy for guiding our actions. From time immemorial men and women have had to act on the best assumptions they could make and, as the fickle finger of fate decrees, sometimes you get it right and sometimes you get it wrong. The question arises as to whether there is ever more than a random distribution of true and false beliefs in terms of expected results in a given population, or with a particular individual over a given period of time. Does high cognitive ability help, and how does this correlate with rationality? The evidence cited in *The Bell Curve* by Herrnstein and Murray suggests that high intelligence does improve the odds of achieving successful outcomes in life, and a component of that is presumably the ability to choose well. Since beliefs of one sort or another are so universal, and the need to believe what someone else says confronts us every day, it is difficult to accept that it is a folk psychology category that will one day disappear and be replaced by a physical description of neuronal processes.

Perhaps the nature of belief is best exemplified by the natural tendency to believe what another person says; to believe what is written in the newspapers, or what is seen in a television documentary programme. We often have no evidence other than the word of the person who is speaking or writing. In such circumstances it is not unreasonable for us to project our own values of integrity and to believe that the other person is employing the same values. If this were not the case, social interchange would take on an immensely more complex character, as everything anyone else said had to be verified before it could be accepted. It is only when we have evidence that another person's word is not to be trusted that we suspend our willingness to believe. Presumably evolution has produced a predisposition to believe that what the other person is saying is what they truly think, even though we may disagree with their point of view. Such belief can hardly be described as having anything to do with rationality because our response is intuitive and subconscious. We do not ask ourselves at every interchange whether the other person is speaking honestly or not. This is why it is often difficult to detect when someone 'speaks with forked tongue'. It seems we have a propensity to believe built into us, and this predisposition can sometimes be readily manipulated by unscrupulous people or those with deeply held beliefs of their own which they wish others to share.

How, then, should we analyse our own beliefs in relation to those we see around us? We can observe beliefs which range from the obsessive and the fanatical to those which are simply an expression of a probable outcome and which can be readily modified should the evidence change. On the whole, society tends to regard belief as laudable, so to be without belief is to be regarded as someone who is rudderless and lacking in conviction. There is social pressure to have clearly held beliefs of some kind rather than to adopt a probabilistic attitude to everything that cannot be known, which would be the more rational stance. There is also an in-built emotional need for belief, presumably as the result of evolutionary pressures. Beliefs offer a shortcut to successful outcomes if they prove to be right, and those who have the beliefs that fit 'the tide in the affairs of men' and act on them come out on top. They are the survivors. But what we are concerned with here is how do we reach our beliefs and what guide do we have in assessing whether they might be valid. Looking around we see such a varied assortment of beliefs we know that they cannot all have the same prob- ability of proving correct in terms of the judgement of history. As we look back 100 years or more it is easier to see who were the visionaries and who were the misguided, but what we want to be able to do is to make that judgement now. This will never be possible on all fronts because we are dealing with the play of chance and the way events turn out is often 'a damn close run thing'. The emergent-algorithm cannot be predicted with any reliability, but there are some things which should be abundantly clear which are not.

If we enter a domain such as politics we cannot reconcile beliefs because they are attached to so many different agendas, many of them being driven by emotional disposition or by social ambition, but in the field of science greater objectivity can be expected because at some time we know there is likely to be a correct answer. The distance we are from a definitive answer will condition the extent to which beliefs have to be employed in under- pinning different theories. On the subject of *mind*, it should be apparent that the final theory is some way away because of the wide disparity of views already displayed in earlier parts of this text. In some ways, exploring the nature of mind can be regarded as an intellectual lottery. To be a player you have to attain a certain state of knowledge and achieve a facility for linguistic expression which allows you to place your bet in a convincing fashion, but in the end you will be displaying a belief which only has a certain level of probability of proving right. Why then does the individual putting forward a belief feel so totally committed to it, even though they must know the odds are against them? Emotional disposition, selective memory and social self-interest all play a part, perhaps disguising any rational appreciation of the situation which may be lurking beneath the public display.

Before we can probe *belief* a little further we need to consider some of the other folk psychology categories, particularly the links between *feelings* and *thought* and the values they generate. There is obviously an emotional content associated with many beliefs, and the rationality content of a particular belief can be quite low. Fear of flying seems to be a good example. Any rational assessment of the statistics associated with flying should reduce concern about the likelihood of a fatal accident to an extremely low level, but at the same time we cannot deny that some planes crash. The belief that our plane might be the one may be irrational, but the feelings associated with the idea can be so strong that a person is inhibited from flying. In this instance the *thought* of flying evokes an emotional response which can trigger the hypothalamus into producing unpleasant bodily sensations via the autonomic nervous system. We can see that here we have a rich interplay of emotion, memory and sensation which rational considerations can do little about unless there is an act of will and a choice to take remedial action. The role of belief in our lives is often deterministic, though the direction belief takes can be altered.

It is obviously going to be quite difficult to reduce belief to a physical neuronal identity, or to devise a replacement physical concept. We would first have to identify the neural correlate of the thought which constitutes the belief, detect any associated memories and relate these to the emotional circuits which are activated and the sensations they produce. On top of this, we would have to determine whether there was any rational overlay. Perhaps a billion or two neurons would be involved at the conscious level, and we then have to take the step of specifying how all this neuronal activity could transform itself into a subjective experience; the feeling of what it is like to believe what we do. We can conclude there is not a ghost of a chance of achieving all this when we haven't yet taken the step of locating the role and nature of belief among all our other conscious experiences, by means of well-controlled population studies. Beliefs have different meanings for each of us, but they would be difficult to prize out by means of language which describes them accurately. Many people would be unwilling to subject themselves to such invasive scrutiny. It is within these limitations that we have to try and make some headway.

Can we be more specific about the areas of the brain employed in belief? Not really, because we can involve most areas in any indicative analysis, and it will depend on the type of belief. A strongly held belief which is adhered to in the face of contradictory views held by others will almost certainly have a significant emotional component. It will generate feelings which support confidence in that belief. The limbic system of the subcortex will be involved, and so will its links with the frontal cortex. But the belief will also require an image or a sequence of words which have to be recalled from memory and integrated with sensations arising from present sensory experience. This will require extensive use of the sensory cortex. There is evidence from split-brain studies (where the corpus callosum has been severed) that the left hemisphere is more involved in the formation of our beliefs than the right hemisphere[3]. But in normal brains it is reasonable to envisage a level of global activity in the brain involving massive emergent-algorithms reverberating through many loops and feedback circuits. What we could do, though, is try and assess the balance between emotion and rationality incorporated into a belief. Is it based on a logical analysis of the possibilities and a considered weighing of the balance of probabilities, or is it an intuitive conviction? Have we an appreciation in our own mind where the balance lies? It should be possible to develop an appropriate psychological scoring technique and then employ modern brain-scanning technology to determine which parts of the brain are most active. There is little doubt that such procedures will be developed which will give us a clearer understanding of the rational and emotional components of belief.

There is also the consideration of whether the propensity to believe varies within populations, and what the effects of that might be. If there is a connection between belief and left-brain activity, as the evidence from Michael Gazzaniga's split-brain work suggests, then it is possible there is an evolutionary connection between language and belief and, perhaps, creative intelligence. A propensity to believe might promote the ability to form inferences which lead to creativity, as well as generating the emotional impulse to act on those inferences. In a highly creative, high-achieving society we then might expect to see widespread belief systems which manifest themselves in a variety of irrational beliefs as well as those based on rational considerations. It would help to explain why so many people hold on to their beliefs, despite contradictory evidence. The subject is obviously a very difficult one to examine in any objective manner. It may be that individual belief is more important than individual rationality for cultural progress, and that the process of rational evaluation is best left to the emergent-algorithms of the cultural group and society at large. If this were the case it would have the unfortunate side effect of promoting a higher degree of outward confusion within society than might otherwise be necessary. It also emphasises that we have a choice to make in the education and training of our children.

When considering belief in the context of animals other than human beings, it becomes even more difficult to decide where the issue stands because of the lack of reportable evidence. When a dog expects his mistress or his master to arrive home, or a fox hunts in a certain area for rabbits, it might be said that they have a belief about likely outcomes. Alternatively, it may simply be feelings that are involved rather than belief. Because of lack of evidence we, more or less, have to confine consideration of belief to human beings, but such is not the case with the next folk psychology category: desire.

Desire

Once again there is a multitude of meanings. A desire can be a momentary wish to satisfy a whim, a basic instinct involving survival of the organism, or a long-term ambition. Like belief, it is an attitude of mind which concerns philosophers and psychologists rather than neuroscientists. Because, like hopes and fears, desire is always directed at a specific object, activity or goal, the philosophers once again classify it as a propositional attitude – a state of affairs which involves *intentionality*. We don't just have desires, we have desires *for* something. Our present concern, however, is more with what is going on in our brain when we exhibit desire rather than any philosophical definition. Clearly, there is a strong emotional component which could well involve the subcortex to an even greater degree than belief. It may even be legitimate to consider desire as a certain type of feeling, though one that can be subject to cognitive evaluation. In the case of sexual desire, for instance, the hypothalamus is known to play a leading role, though careful reflection may lead us to conclude that this is neither the time nor the place for a particular impulse, and it is soon suppressed. When the hypothalamus signals hunger it is not so easy to push the desire to the back of our minds, and we usually construct ways of satisfying it. As human beings we become conscious of our desires, though the degree to which we analyse them varies enormously.

It might be useful to consider desire in a less fundamental context, and for that we need a specific example. Let's consider the statement, 'I have a desire to get out of here'. One of the first questions to arise is how strong is that desire? It may be that I simply want to go home for tea, or it could be that I feel trapped and incarcerated. If I am claustrophobic and stuck in a lift there could be a sense of overwhelming panic. However we grade the level of desire, it is difficult to dissociate it from some kind of emotional state. This is also likely to be true for non-human species, so that a fox hearing the baying of hounds will experience fear, and a desire to be somewhere else. Immediate evasive action results. A desire 'to get out of here' really starts at the level of sensation and it probably arises in the first instance because of an external or internal stimulus. It may be too hot, or there is an unpleasant smell, or it may be that I have become bored because there is insufficient sensory stimulus. A notable characteristic of human beings is a desire to have their conscious hours occupied in a way that produces emotional satisfaction. If the place I am in does not provide sufficient stimulus then it is likely I will develop a desire to be elsewhere. For this to happen the sensations my brain is receiving, or not receiving, must react with knowledge of what might be available elsewhere, and so invoke memory.

Sensations, emotions and memory are all involved in my desire to 'get out of here'. Up to this point of analysis we haven't employed any faculties which are uniquely human. The baying of hounds produces a particular sensation in the fox because he has a memory of what it means. If he had no memory, why worry? It is unlikely he can reflect on his desire 'to get out of here' and that he responds to an overwhelming feeling. This fundamental role of *feeling* is something we will meet time and time again, to such an extent that we will have to consider it as a basic property of consciousness, perhaps *the* basic property.

If we assume I want to 'get out of here' because I need a drink and then I reflect that my thirst is not all that bad and that the pubs will be open in an hour, I might decide to wait. It seems unlikely that a fox can possibly have the concept of 'waiting an hour', since that is a sophisticated calculation for which I am indebted to past generations and my own learned experience. After all, I did not devise the concept of an hour. Language and rational deliberation have entered into my mental processes, which cause me to suppress my desire for the time being, though I will keep looking at my watch with some impatience. We have now involved all five mental variables mentioned at the end of Chapter 2 in this simple act of desiring, even though some of them are mainly involved in qualifying the nature of the desire. I can only speculate on the essential difference between myself and the fox, but I would hazard a guess that it centres around the conscious awareness of desire. Perhaps it is even wrong to attribute desire of any sort to a fox if he cannot become consciously aware of it, and we should leave his sensations, memory and emotions in the sphere of an instinct based on feeling. That is a semantic quibble I will not bother to take any further, because there is no means of resolving it and we are essentially concerned with the human condition.

In breaking down the nature of desire we can see that there is a hierarchy of mental processes. The basic layout of our sensory nervous system is shared with many other animals, though the way we interpret sensory stimuli may be quite different. One obvious difference is that we seem to be in much greater need of stimulus than lower-order species, and it is much more likely that I will want 'to get out of here' because of boredom than will a fox. In fact, the demand that human consciousness makes for nourishment seems to be one of the driving forces of the species. If we didn't have the need to fill our waking hours with interesting activity it is likely that the achievements of *Homo sapiens* would be of a much lower order. Perhaps the main difference between achievers and non-achievers in this world is the level at which this appetite of consciousness for time-filling rewards becomes satiated. There are, of course, well proven ways of controlling this appetite, and spiritual meditation is one that immediately comes to mind. The employment of techniques to suppress desire can bring peace of mind to the individual. If this leads to a passive state, then the question of whether or not there is a net gain by society depends on whether the individual's unconstrained desires would otherwise have had a negative or a positive impact. The act of dampening down antisocial desires would seem to be an obvious goal for all of us but, perhaps, those with an excess of such desires are the least likely to undertake a course on monastic meditation.

Desire that is self-centred and largely untempered by concern for others has a lot to answer for in determining the acceptability of social behaviour. If we play our 'population distribution game' once again we could plot a bell-shaped curve using an index for 'the degree of concern for others', with, at one end of the axis, a total lack of concern (sociopathic behaviour) to, at the other end, an almost complete dedication to the interests of others (altruistic behaviour). Then we might speculate about what produces these different dispositions, and orientation of desire will certainly feature prominently. What this means in terms of neuronal circuits is likely to remain a mystery for a long, long time, but as a working framework we can envisage that the interplay between centres in the subcortex and sensory cortex are modified by modulating influences from the frontal cortex and the more advanced centres of the sensory cortex where language is processed. For many activities of the brain we can regard the subcortex as the energising centre, but it is doubtful if it actually triggers operations. It is true that simple electrical stimulation of the hypothalamus and other parts of the limbic system can produce a variety of psychological states: anguish, despair, euphoria, sexual desire, depending on the part stimulated; but this is clearly the result of an external stimulus. It seems reasonable to assume that, in normal circumstances, an external event needs to trigger a sensation, or an internal stimulus has to arise from a cerebral event involving memory.

The limbic system represents the emotional core of the brain. It consists of a number of structures composed of grey matter, including the hippocampus, the hypothalamus, the amygdala, and the cingulate gyrus (which is buried in the inner, white matter areas of the temporal lobes). The whole group of structures sits centrally and towards the base of the cerebral hemispheres. As well as having a complex network of neuronal connections with the rest of the brain, it is subject to the influence of a variety of neurotransmitters and a medley of hormones released through the agency of the hypothalamus, which can influence cell metabolism and the production of all those peptides and proteins that neurons are constantly manufacturing. With this sort of complexity it is little wonder that it is so difficult to work out exactly what is going on, but pieces of the jigsaw will gradually emerge as the use of investigatory techniques and pharmacological agents becomes more specific. We have recently seen with 'Prozac' and related drugs that inhibition of the re-uptake of 5-hydroxytryptamine into presynaptic terminals of neurons in the limbic system can lead to a calming and equilibratory effect on behaviour.

I have already referred to the strong link between desire and emotion, and this makes it opportune to look a little more closely at the nature of emotion and to break it down into two broad categories – the *inner* and *outer* aspects of emotional experience. Most of us have no difficulty in recognising if people are being 'emotional' because they exhibit a certain type of behaviour. They may be frightened, angry, infatuated, overjoyed, hysterical or in one of many other possible states. Their demeanour will provide strong clues as to which. But there are other emotions which are outwardly masked and which are virtually impossible to discern by observation. These are hidden within the inner experience of the person and are commonly referred to as *feelings*. Antonio Damasio has distinguished very clearly between 'feelings' and 'emotions', and has reserved the expression *feelings* to describe longer term mental dispositions which are generally confined to the inner space of the individual[4]. Emotion in its 'outer' manifestation can be regarded as an acute change in body state which is induced by a powerful mental surge involving subcortical structures. Feelings are much more subtle and are generally lower keyed. They are tailored to the individual and are more complex than the well-pronounced emotional reactions programmed into our subcortex. Examples that follow will help to clarify the situation.

Feelings

The *Oxford Companion to the Mind* lists *feelings* in its index and says: 'see emotion; sensations'[5]. There is clearly a good deal of terminological overlap in common usage of these words so it would be unwise to be too pedantic in our use of the terms. Perhaps an example will best indicate the major sense in which I would like to employ *feeling*, and for that I need to resort to my own experience. I have an emotional predisposition to stay put where I am living or working, rather than to fly around the world on holidays or sightseeing expeditions as some people do. This may seem surprising to those who know me because I have lived in Japan and the United States, and have travelled widely, including a 5000-mile car trip across the United States. Such excursions have always been determined by the dictates of my job. I have never resisted travel and have been happy to 'go with the flow', but left totally to my own preferences, I do not travel unless there is a special reason. Forty years ago, during my National Service, when I was in charge of the medical stores at the Cambridge Military Hospital, Aldershot, it was part of my duties to travel around the medical centres of the various barracks to check inventories of medical equipment. I never enjoyed doing that, preferring to work at base. When I handed over to my successor at the end of my service, he was only too keen to jump in a jeep and to start his visits. That memory has stayed strongly with me, so it must have some significance. Despite all the travel in those intervening years, my basic predisposition hasn't changed. Even though I am retired and could holiday abroad as much as I like, the prospect doesn't appeal. I could rationalise that by saying that I find hotel rooms sterile and I prefer to have the benefit of my full-frequency-range music systems at home, but it is something more deep seated than that. It is better described as a feeling rather than an emotion, and it affects the way I plan my life.

I suppose the foundations were laid sometime in my childhood, but I am unable to identify where, when or how. It seems unlikely that it is something built into my genes. Although I recall my childhood as essentially a happy one, we certainly didn't travel very much, and when we did it was to relatives. We did not have a car, and I did not own a bicycle until much later than my friends: I can remember running to keep up with them. I was nearly five years old when the Second World War started. I remember the bombs falling in London, and listening to the engines stop on the doodle-bugs, but I cannot recall ever feeling any sense of fear. My sister and I were evacuated twice, but only for a few months each time. In those days we used to wander far and wide, there being no traffic to speak of and no fear of crime. I remember playing football in the park at 11 o'clock at night in double summer time, so I was hardly restricted in my movements. There are many people who had a childhood similar to mine who love to travel, so where did my particular feelings come from? I have no idea, but wherever they arose they are peculiar to me, and obviously not something programmed into the basic emotional structure of everybody's brain. If we were to play our population distribution game based on the distance people had travelled during their lives, I suppose I would find myself well down the right-hand slope of the bell-shaped distribution curve, but if we measured the propensity to travel for the sheer pleasure of doing so, it would be quite a different matter. This would not be obvious from external examination. Each of us has his own particular feelings locked away and hidden, though some are more prepared to declare them than others.

Antonio Damasio puts forward a hypothesis as to how the neural networks in the brain might work with regard to feelings. He places a lot of emphasis on the prefrontal cortices in the cerebral hemispheres. These are the anterior (right at the front) parts of the frontal lobes. He draws these inferences from the way some of his patients with prefrontal damage (like Phineas Gage) think and behave and he cites experimental evidence to support the observation that there is an emotional deficit in such patients. Initially, this might seem surprising because we think of the subcortex as the emotional centre, with the amygdala and the hypothalamus playing a key role, but we should never tire of reminding ourselves that inter-connections in the brain are extremely complex. Damasio goes further than this though and invokes what he calls *somatic markers* – reactions and feedback from the body which tell us what our emotions are. This is related to the role of the autonomic nervous system which I have already referred to several times. We should note there are reservations about this point of view within the scientific community. William James, as long as a century ago, postulated that all emotions resulted from bodily events mediated through the autonomic nervous system, but eminent biologists were later to show that animals were fully capable of emotional behaviour when all their nerves to and from the body were severed. Allan Hobson describes patients feeling anxiety and fear in their dreams during REM sleep[6], when all bodily sensations are blocked off in the brain stem. These difficulties can be circumvented if we remind ourselves that the brain stores mapped repre-sentations of the body and has an acquired memory of its physiological characteristics. Evidence of the remarkable powers of the brain and the deceptive tricks it can play have already been mentioned in connection with the sensory cortex (Chapter 1). Perhaps the most telling example in this context is the phantom-limb phenomenon, where someone who has had a limb amputated can still feel phantom pains associated with a precise condition in the phantom limb. Damasio postulates that, in certain condi-tions, the brain can activate cortical, limbic and brain stem nuclei which totally bypass the body but give the same feeling *as if* the autonomic nervous system had been activated. He calls these 'as if' loops. We do not have to try and resolve exactly which circuits are in play for any given feeling, but each of us should be able to determine for ourselves where our most typical feelings seem to be sited.

We can proceed on the basis that there are prefrontal networks which activate the amygdala and hypothalamus and, hence, the autonomic nervous system and the endocrine system. There is evidence from a number of workers that the right-hemisphere is dominant in the processing of emotion, and this may be another example of evolution deciding that for one part of the brain, 'the buck stops here'. In terms of the variables we have been considering, it soon becomes clear that they are all involved. If I think about travel it may be because I have seen or heard something that produces a *sensation*, and here I am thinking of a sensation as more of a perception than a feeling. (See the trouble language can get us into, though we will try some clarification later!) My mind is aware that the subject of attention is travel, and the fact that it is aware is because my visual or auditory centres have picked up a stimulus. Of course, the stimulus may have been entirely internal and come from *memory* because I have been in a reflective mood and my mind has been wandering over various subjects. Immediately I am consciously aware of an image involving travel being processed in my temporal and occipital lobes, my frontal cortex starts to evaluate the position and checks with the nuclei in my limbic system about how I feel on the matter. Not too keen, they signal. So my frontal lobes start to *rationalise* the situation and try to decide whether there is a good reason for me to travel to achieve a specific objective or simply to obtain the pleasure of the experience. In my case, the latter reasoning is given short shrift. It would be difficult to go through this process without some resort to *language* in the mental imagery.

If I were an agoraphobic, the mere thought of travelling outside my home would stimulate emotions so strong that I would cancel the idea of any such adventure. Everyone can recognise that emotions of this nature are irrational, though the agoraphobic is unable to overcome the emotional signals without effort and guidance. This is an example of extreme dominance of our emotional system, which can manifest itself in a multitude of different phobias. Clearly, this is beyond the realm of *feelings* because the emotions are too strong to warrant such a passive description. However, at a lower level of influence, feelings can and do guide our lives, and I am confident that I will have the vast majority of readers on my side in making this assertion. It would certainly be possible to do some philosophical nit-picking on this contention, but an essentialist analysis really wouldn't get us very far because the only way to resolve the matter would be to institute a properly controlled population study, if it were possible to design such a study in a satisfactory manner.

Whether feelings are pleasant or unpleasant to us as individuals will have an important influence on the way we behave, but it is difficult to get a firm grip on the matter because we all respond in different ways. We surely all seek feelings that are pleasurable rather than the reverse, but we might get into trouble trying to define a pleasant feeling. *Rewarding* might be a better term, because some people seem to get satisfaction from experiences which seem distinctly unpleasant to others. It is not going too far to assert that, for most of us, feelings are the guiding influences in our lives, and yet we do not know how to categorise or how to measure them. What scale should we use in plotting the distribution of feelings across the population? Since we would have to rely on the verbal reports of individuals, and many people are unable to categorise their feelings accurately, if indeed any of us are, it is a difficult issue to resolve. We all know what it is to have *'feelings of'* a certain kind and, to get us going, it might be useful to list a few positives and negatives:

Positive	*Negative*
adequacy	inadequacy
elation	despair
excitement	boredom
contentment	discontentment
calmness	anxiety
confidence	insecurity
importance	insignificance
fulfilment	emptiness

As with any such list of words there are overlaps and ambiguities in meaning, and it might be argued they do not all fall into the same category since some are purely subjective dispositions (e.g. contentment) and others relate to reactive states of some kind (e.g. fulfilment). Semantics can lead us down all sorts of tortuous routes, but we do not need to be side-tracked by such considerations, because the only question I want to raise is, 'Do these descriptions all represent different physiological and mental states or are they all routes to degrees of the same thing?' Obviously, some represent stronger emotional states than others, so that *elation* is different in degree to *calmness*, and *despair* to *boredom*, but can they be regarded as underlying neurophysiological states of a different kind, and if so what are the differences? The fact is that nobody can really answer this question. There are some general ideas about which parts of the brain and nervous system are involved in emotions and feelings, but most people probably do not care too much whether it is their amygdala, hypothalamus, cingulate gyrus, autonomic nervous system, prefrontal cortex or a mixture of the lot. What they would prefer to know is how to turn negative feelings into positive ones without having to transport themselves into a different life situation. In fact, the negative feelings which produce much unhappiness are often blamed on external circumstances rather than any internal disposition. They may be attributed to difficulties in the family, problems at work, trouble with friends and yet have neurotransmitter and hormonal imbalance as their real cause. How much grief might be avoided if people could be taught how to examine their own internal state in the first instance?

But, back to our population-distribution picture and the bell-shaped curve. Given the complexities surrounding feelings, what measure can we use for the sorts of feelings which guide our day-to-day actions, those that produce a sense of contentment and satisfaction or their converse? They relate to our work, the people we share our lives with, where we live, the extent to which we are absorbed by our interests, and the way the great, wide world impinges on our lives. Many factors are beyond our direct control and yet we react to all of them by generating feelings of some kind. Quite often the reaction is fairly neutral, sometimes (perhaps quite rarely) it is a sense of joy. At other times there is a sense of apprehension or distress. We can keep generating words and more words to describe these feelings until we come to the conclusion that the philosophers who want to eliminate folk psychology descriptions must have a point: these words don't give us much of a clue about what is going on in the underlying neurophysiological processes. As a working basis I am going to assume (along with Antonio Damasio) that our autonomic nervous systems are a crucial component in signalling the way we feel; that the activity of our prefrontal cortices, amygdalas, hypothalami, etc express themselves in the bodily sensations we experience through our parasympathetic and sympathetic nervous systems. Without these bodily sensations we would not have to worry much about feelings. For each of us the menu of sensations will be different, as will the stimuli that produce them, so it would be senseless to try and provide a universal formulation. For our hypothetical population study I am going to employ a scale of 1 to 7, running from *negative autonomic feeling* to *positive autonomic feeling*, with each person making their own judgement where they stand after we have carefully explained the concept to them and enabled them to interpret their own somatic experiences.

I remember once saying to a colleague, 'I don't have moods', which wasn't strictly true of course, but it did make a valid point, since my mood fluctuations were far narrower than the highs and the lows I observed around me. In other words I tend to hover around 4 on the scale of 1 to 7. I am fortunate in largely avoiding the pits of 1, but deprived in that I have rarely experienced 7, and the opportunities to do so seem to recede in direct proportion to age. The pinnacles around 7 are probably scaled with youth and love, but such ecstatic experiences seldom last very long. Those who have suffered severe depression or who have had to confront a phobia will know about 1. In constructing our population distribution curve we could take a snapshot at a particular moment in time, because of the variation within individuals over time. A manic-depressive personality will tend to fluctuate widely between extremes and more equable temperaments less so. However, if each of us were to judge our mean score over the past year, we

could plot that. Now, here's the crunch. What chance do we have of favour-
ably modifying our mean score on autonomic feelings, given that they are
dependent to a large extent on neuronal networks in our brains working in a
soup of neurotransmitters and hormones? Drugs, therapeutic and otherwise,
are often employed, but that seems a bit of a cop-out and nasty side-effects
can result in the long term. Meditative techniques have helped many people,
but they need a lot of concentration and tend to take you out of circulation.
Have you ever tried to hold a conversation with someone meditating? For
the majority of us there has to be another way. One thing is pretty certain, if
you do not understand what is happening to yourself, you are likely to
blame others for your condition to an inappropriate extent.

   Things will go wrong as often as they go right for most of us because of
the inherent uncertainty of predicting external forces and the way they will
influence the future. If everything is going right, no problem. It is when
events proceed in a contrary direction to our desires, or clash with our
values and beliefs, that we feel that unpleasant twinge somewhere in our
gut, chest, or musculature and we need to call on the resources of our
prefrontal cortices as the part of our nervous system most amenable to
conscious deliberation. If Damasio is right, that the ventro-medial area of
the prefrontal cortices is directly involved in assessing and modulating our
feelings, then it should be possible to employ it to our advantage. Of course,
it will need will-power and the effort necessary to modify those conditioned
emotional responses, but if its resources are employed at the first signals of
distress it should be possible to modify the overall CNS response. How it is
done will vary from individual to individual, but the first essential is to
recognise what is happening. The frequent use of both CNS stimulants and
depressants (including alcohol) to aid this task suggests that people are
likely to respond in radically different ways to their typical 'feeling down'
syndrome, so there is unlikely to be a universal remedy. We have to search
for our own. Sometimes a counter-irritant strategy may be the most
effective line of attack, through engaging in activity which may not be
particularly rewarding in itself but diverts our attention from the cause of
the negative feeling. For many this could be strenuous physical exercise. On
another occasion a frontal assault on those negative autonomic signals will
be called for, by adopting behaviour which is contrary to the way you feel;
like singing in the shower. Another way is to ignore the feelings, and
behave as though they did not exist. None of these options is easy, and I
mention them only to illustrate that there are avenues open to us which we
can try, to see how efficacious they are. As with most rewarding tasks,
persistence is needed.

   It would be extremely arrogant of us as human beings to assume that feelings were confined to our species. Dogs have been described as man's best friend and this species provides the most familiar example of a non-human animal showing evidence of feelings. Their delight at being taken for a walk or being petted is evident to every dog owner. How can we envisage their brain mechanisms operating? Since they do not have the benefit of language they are probably unable to form concepts in the way we can, and they show little evidence of self-awareness. This doesn't prevent the possibility of them having mental images. They have a sensory cortex and can see and hear, and their sense of smell is much better developed than our own. What does a particular scent mean to a dog? Does it produce a sensory image or is it merely connected to a particular feeling which arises through memory of that scent? We cannot, of course, answer these questions, but it is possible to envisage a model of mental activity which is dependent purely on feelings to guide action. I would like to describe this as the *default model*. In the absence of definitive evidence we can work on the assumption that feelings alone are capable of determining action. In our own instance we are able to undertake complex thought processes, and it is possible in principle to act on the basis of a rational evaluation of those thought processes. But, I would venture, that when we come to translate our thought processes into action, most of us rely on our feelings for guidance. In fact, many of our likes and dislikes are beyond rational assessment.

The food we eat and the music we listen to provide two of the most illustrative examples of how our feelings dominate. A nutritious diet could be designed for each and everyone of us, based on the best scientific evidence. Not many would be willing to stick to such a diet because each of us derives pleasure from different sorts of food. My own taste buds have a predilection for Chinese food, and I would feel deprived if I could not have my weekly fix. There are people, I believe, who would not relish such a regular exposure to oriental cuisine. One of the world's great tastes, in my opinion, is raw fish accompanied by soy sauce and wasabi. Many would react with horror at the thought. Millions of Americans enjoy a weak percolation of coffee, whereas I will only drink Expresso. Obviously, there is no prospect of rational resolution of these differences based on a theoretical, idealised diet. In the case of music there isn't even a biological imperative. For some people, no music is better than any music. An attempt to promote the merits of Wagner to a devotee of ZZ Top is likely to be wasted, though I happen to like both. The quality of the sound matters to some and is a question of total indifference to others. My own sensitivity to sound means I often have to operate the 'off' switch on radio programmes where mono-recordings are transmitted or when an ancient forte piano is employed in a broadcast recital.

How these preferences develop has nothing much to do with rationality but they can certainly be the subject of rational study. Whether feelings develop through the expression of a genetically determined selection mechanism in the brain, or whether they emerge because of an environmental instruction programme which results in the formation of specific neuronal networks, is a matter which is likely to occupy scientists for many years to come. In the meantime I would like to employ *feelings* at the centre of my default model, a model which can be reshaped and modified as new evidence appears. In this model the subcortex is central to feelings. I have already indicated that there is strong evidence for non-human animals having feelings, without the need to employ the services of a human neo-cortex. No one would deny that a human infant under two years of age has feelings, despite the fact that many higher cerebral circuits are not yet in place. Although the infant has more neurons and more synapses than an adult, it has not yet developed its cognitive circuits or its memory networks. Nevertheless, the infant brain has to control homeostasis through the brain stem, the somatic and autonomic nervous system and the body's endocrine glands. There are thousands of metabolic systems under this central control, and the aggregate effect is to give a sense of body state, body function and body image on which all externally derived sensations impinge. It can be viewed as the conscious balance sheet of the organism, comprised of credits and debits of feeling.

In any large, international organisation there is an incredible variety of activity, and in the end it all gets summarised in the balance sheet and the profit or loss statement. The term *balance sheet* has a nice, harmonious ring to it and it is a legitimate way of summarising an organisation's perform-ance. Cash flow is often more important than notional profit in describing the financial health of the organisation. In order to get a measure of financial health, the accountancy system has to penetrate all activities and measure the relevant expenditure and income. It doesn't have to understand all those activities, like research and development for instance, but it has to integrate financial aspects of those activities with quite unrelated parts of the organisation. Using this picture as an analogy for a living organism we have to look for a structure or a system which can link disparate parts together. Such a candidate is the subcortex of the brain. It is, after all, connected to everything, just like those accountants!

When we think of human cognitive activity we tend to concentrate on the neocortex because it is quite clearly involved in higher order thought and it has specialised regions concerned with sensory experience, motor perform-ance and linguistic competence. As the neocortex develops its neural circuits and its cognitive powers in the human infant it is in many ways convenient to regard these as essentially computational in nature. Such an approach has led to many of the developments in artificial intelligence and the construction of electronic networks which can simulate aspects of sensory experience and cognition. But whatever computational circuits are laid down they eventually have to make a decision about what action the organism should take. It would be nice to think, in the case of human beings, that such decisions were always entirely rational, but we know that is hardly ever the case. There is never enough information for us to demonstrate with logical certainty that we have got it right, and experience tells us that half the population will disagree with us whatever we do. We have to resort to our beliefs, and the feelings on which they are based, in order to make a decision. In the domain of emotional decision-making the subcortex has an important role. The feelings generated by the interaction of subcortex and neocortex are centre stage in our conscious experience and they are there in the background to all our thoughts. It is *thought* that we will examine in the next chapter.

Chapter 4

Factors Influencing Thought

Population Factors

Thought can be distinguished from feelings in that it has specific content which can be described in terms readily understood by others. There is no need for neurophysiological or psychological description. Both feelings and thoughts have the attribute of being consciously available to us, and although there are probably elements of both which are unconscious, it is the conscious aspects which most concern us. Consciousness makes feelings and thoughts accessible and provides the means by which we recognise an experience. The nature of consciousness is intimately tied up with both, and since conscious experience is still a central mystery of mind, we will have to adopt a working framework in order to proceed with an analysis. Suppose, for the moment, we think of the neocortex of the brain as a processor of information with two sorts of input: internal and external. The internal inputs make us what we are as individuals because they depend on the physiology of our nervous system and how it connects up with the architecture of our organs and our tissues. The way these interact is governed by a sea of hormones, autacoids, neurotransmitters, peptides and proteins. We should not forget that our neurons operate in this chemical soup, which is genetically laid down for the species but which will vary significantly from individual to individual, giving each of us our unique fingerprint.

This genetically determined composition, with its epigenetic modifications, dictates the way we process external information, which will always be modulated to some degree by the time it springs into conscious consideration. To make my point clearer it may be helpful to use the analogy of the reproduction of a symphony concert in a hi-fi system. No matter how close your system gets to the original sound, there will always be subtle differences to what was heard in the concert hall, so that in the final analysis no two hi-fi systems will ever sound exactly the same. Indeed, even if we are sitting in the concert hall, the precise formation of sound waves impinging on our ears will differ in some degree to those arriving at any other pair of ears. We know from chaos theory that minute differences in initial conditions (in this case the sound waves arriving at the ears) can result in enormous differences in the final state of the system. This is commonly known as the *butterfly effect*, with the flapping of a hypothetical butterfly's wings over Beijing causing perturbations in the prevailing air stream sufficient to result in a gale over New York when it arrives there. In the case of sound being perceived by the human brain, it is not just differences in the wiring and the quality of the components that we have to contend with, but all those memories built up over the years and the feelings they generate. We do not come off a standardised production line.

It is here that any essentialist analysis of thought has to falter, because that analysis, even if it were carried out with impeccable exactitude, can only represent the person carrying out the analysis. It may produce an admirable work of philosophical or psychoanalytical art, but there is nothing to demonstrate that it has any special meaning for the population as a whole. To generate a scientific theory of thought we would have to carry out a population study, and you can see immediately that this presents serious difficulties. How do we even approach a controlled study of thought, let alone one that would meet the elementary conditions we would expect for investigating a new drug acting on the central nervous system – a randomised, double-blind study? Let's go back to our symphony concert. The fact that we are there listening to the music must surely mean that mental processes ensue which can be categorised as thought. I suppose there are people who might react to music on the basis of pure feeling but it seems reasonable to assume that most members of the audience at a Mahler concert will process mental images of some sort during the course of the performance. These images will wander in and out and make various connections, say, with the admirable profile of the conductor, that pretty young lady in the second violins, and the awful acoustic of the new concert hall. This is not to imply that there are no people in the audience who concentrate on the notes all the time! These images and thoughts are formed over a period of time, quite a lot of time in the case of a Mahler symphony, and if we were to try and analyse them we would be faced by daunting complexity. If we now take the two thousand people in the audience and try to identify a common denominator, it would be difficult to locate one even if we had a process with which we could make a start. Just imagine those billions of neurons in each brain, some involved in consciousness, others not, disgorging their neurotransmitters at their trillions of synaptic terminals and linking up in millions of different circuits, or in whatever way they form those images which constitute conscious thought. In any case, it is quite probable that these neural impulses only have meaning in the context of the background of each individual and there is no external measure which can be used to find a common denominator.

But one redeeming feature about most complex adaptive systems is that they have an observable outcome. We might not know exactly what has caused it to rain in New York, or in what way that butterfly disturbed those molecules of oxygen and nitrogen 7000 miles away, but we can observe that it is raining. In the case of our concert there will be a consensus view about the performance, if we take the trouble to find out. This outcome is the result of an emergent-algorithm. Every individual has processed his or her experiences over a period of two hours with an immensely complex set of neural firings and ends up with an assessment that can be reported on when asked. If we then take the 2000 concert goers we can employ statistical techniques to determine an overall opinion on the performance. We will have to use a highly standardised procedure if the results are to be of any value. I don't know whether you have ever participated in one of those conferences where the audience rates the speakers, but, if you have, and you study the comments received afterwards, the chances are you will begin to wonder whether everybody was at the same event. Any population study is bound to show, I confidently predict, what immensely different thought processes we all have, though we can use statistical techniques to get a general impression of their distribution.

How does this arise? If we all witness the same event isn't it reasonable to expect a common interpretation? It would certainly make it a lot easier if the thoughts forming our judgements were shared by everyone else. Think of all the disagreement we could avoid. We either have to assume that we are each injected with a different spiritual essence by some agency with a perverse sense of discord, or that our brains have simply developed differ-ently. This latter possibility is not difficult to envisage considering the degree of complexity involved and the vastly different experiences our brains have been exposed to during their lifetime. When we consider our own mental processes we are intuitively aware of our indebtedness to our earlier experiences and that our mind would not be what it is now without our particular history of sensory stimuli. Of course, that experience has to work on a substrate, and that substrate differs for each of us because of differences in genetic constitution. This combination of nature and nurture provides us with our own unique thought machine and ensures we don't think quite like anybody else.

We are now at the crux of our problem. How do we set about interpreting the thought processes of others? A good place to start is trying to understand our own. Even though we cannot reliably use our own thought processes as a template for judging another mind, it might be helpful in identifying points of departure. Before we start any folk psychology analysis, it is worth reminding ourselves of Gerald Edelman's theory that the brain is dynamically organised into populations of neurons, called *neuronal groups*, which have been selected during development by the way in which they have been stimulated by both internal and external inputs. The principle of 'use it, or lose it' can be said to apply to any particular neuronal group, because if it is used the synapses become strengthened and if it isn't, they weaken. The more often and the longer a neuronal group is used the more firmly preserved is its encoding. These neuronal groups link up to form networks or maps, which again depend on use in determining how solidly they are established, and the facility with which they will respond to re-entrant signals. Many of these neuronal groups work in parallel, so that if, for any reason, a particular group fails, others can take over its role, so that we have a dynamically and statistically controlled system. It should be remembered that up to 70% of neurons can die during development, and while there are no doubt stochastic factors at play, those with an active role stand the best chance of survival. While the principle of neuronal group selection applies throughout life, it is particularly important during growth and development when the 'primary repertoires' are established. All this is hypothesis, but it gives us a useful model to explain why even genetically identical twins are unlikely to have identical wiring, let alone you and your boss.

Whether we will ever be able to say what constitutes a particular thought is probably as open a question as whether it will be possible to define consciousness. In fact, it has been said that consciousness is nothing more than the process of thought, though I think this is a point of view we need to challenge. We can speculate that there are topographically organised neuronal groups firing away and arranged into global maps, but how does this constitute a thought which enters into conscious awareness, and how is a particular thought selected? Is it something to do with emergence in a complex system, is quantum coherence involved, can it be explained by one of many 'multiple drafts' coming to the fore, as Daniel Dennett thinks[1], or is there some mysterious ghost in the machine? None of these ideas seems to have gripped the imagination on a wide scale because evidence is lacking. For the moment we are left with a folk psychology approach, and with its aid and a little help from the philosophers we can break thought down into components which seem to be an essential part of the process. It would be presumptuous to suggest a definitive list, but my own shortlist for analysis is:

1. Time
2. Attention
3. Perception
4. Memory

5.   Language
6.   Emotion
7.   Cognition

Even this limited number of variables presents a formidable challenge in trying to assess what is going on, but let's see how far we can progress.

Time

Time is fundamental to thought in the sense that all thoughts have to be structured over a period of time. Even a moment of inspiration occupies a finite amount of time. All of us have an innate sense of the flow of time, though physicists and mathematicians have demonstrated that time is much more mysterious than it appears on the surface. The essential question that we have to consider is how it impinges on consciousness. Investigators have convincingly demonstrated that many of our actions take place before we can be consciously aware of them, as happens in the case of the return of a tennis serve. It takes between 5 and 10 milliseconds for a neuron to fire, but between 300 and 700 milliseconds for us to become conscious of an event. In that time a vast array of firing patterns can have swept across the cortex and subcortex. Of course, there are many neuronal firing patterns that never reach consciousness, and one of the most intriguing questions about the mind is what determines whether a thought reaches conscious awareness.

Awareness of time seems to vary quite dramatically between individuals. We all know people who seem to have little sense of time and arrive at the airport just as the boarding gates are closing, whereas others have found it necessary to be there two hours beforehand. The world is divided into the early arrivers and the late arrivers; there are the minute counters and those who are oblivious to the hours, yet our underlying physiology is more or less the same. I have never heard of anyone who doesn't get the desired impression from a movie with still pictures running at a rate of 25 frames per second. Slowing down of mental processes occurs with age and, of course, time perspective tends to become more compressed as events are viewed within a longer life span. Perhaps this is why we oldies are in less need of entertainment and diversionary experiences. Generally, we can only think of one thing at a time, so thought can be regarded as a serial process where queuing is necessary for neural events to enter conscious awareness. Evidence for this comes from our attempts to think our own thoughts at the same time as listening to someone else's conversation. We can sometimes manage it for a short period, but inevitably it soon becomes apparent, at least to ourselves, that our mind is wandering, and we frantically try and tune in again to what the other person is saying.

When we consider attention and perception we have to bear in mind that it takes time for these processes to work. The neural firing patterns which are involved will often be referred to as *neural maps*, for want of a better term, but these are not static displays in the way we normally think of maps. They are ever changing dynamic patterns which may be non-linear in nature and which may only have meaning when reacting with the individual's own internal system, so that any external interpretation is impossible. So far, after many years of research, no neuroscientist has been able to identify patterns of neural firing which are associated with specific sensations in any subject, human or non-human. This has to be differentiated from the more amenable, macroscopic task of pin-pointing areas of the brain which are active during particular mental activity. Don't forget, there can be up to 100 000 neurons per cubic millimetre of neocortex[2].

Attention

Whenever we are conscious our attention tends to be focussed on just one of a number of possible subjects. We may concentrate on the subject at hand for a considerable time or we may flit from one thing to another. It does seem that there is a central channel in the brain which allows us to select only one sensory input at a time, though we may switch channels pretty rapidly. Evidence provided by Donald Broadbent in the late 1950s indicated that we can switch attention no more than twice a second[3]. His claim seems to have stood the test of time, since it correlates well with the 500 milliseconds (approximately) that modern studies suggest it takes to become conscious of an event. This does not mean that our single channel of consciousness blocks out all other signals entirely because most of us can attest to being aware of events at the periphery of our attention, even if only vaguely. This certainly accords with my own experience. I always listen to music while I read, though it may be something of an illusion that I am paying attention to both. A deficit becomes apparent if I try to listen to speech at the same time as reading and try to fully understand the content of both. When I was a lot younger I used to pride myself in writing my best reports while watching television. I certainly find that impossible to achieve now and it makes me wonder whether the faster switching speed of youth made the illusion of multiple channels possible.

There is a good deal of evidence that subcortical nuclei are involved in the attention mechanism, with the thalamus playing an important role. The basal ganglia and the limbic system, with their links to the frontal cortex, have also been implicated. Neuropsychologists have observed that frontal lobe damage can impair the attentional system, producing increased distractibility and difficulty in grasping the whole of a complicated state of affairs. This may well be connected with a deficit in working memory located in the frontal cortex. Since attention involves maintaining consciousness of a subject over a period of time, it becomes necessary to correlate the sensory experience of the present moment with the one that occurred a second or so ago, in order to produce a sense of continuity. We then have to add in any stored, longer-term memories which may be associated with the object under attention and any cognitive analysis that takes place as a consequence. All this neuronal activity has to be bound together so that we can have a seamless conscious experience, and it may be in this regard that the nuclei of the thalamus become vitally important. There is a body of opinion that regular oscillations of neural firings at a frequency of 40 Hz, which originate in the intralaminar nucleus (ILN) of the thalamus and are transmitted via the reticular nucleus, provide the temporal binding mechanism for selective attention. There is no doubt that the ILN is essential for consciousness because bilateral damage of this tiny area of the brain results in unconsciousness. This contrasts with consciousness being maintained despite damage to large tracts of the neocortex.

If the thalamus does prove to be the orchestrator of attention, it provides an ancient mechanism in the brain which we share with many other species. As the predator stalks its prey and the potential victim constantly watches and listens for danger, they are employing sensory pathways which are processed in their thalami before passing on to their cortices, and the feedback loops between thalamus and cortex will be highly active. Next time you are aware of the unwanted attention of a colleague in the office you at least have the option of appealing to their higher centres and asking them to switch their thalamocortical circuits to matters more pertinent to their own business. Given the evolutionary basis of attention mechanisms in the brain it is perhaps not so surprising after all that many people cannot resist prying into the affairs of others. They may not be a whiz at their own job, but they always feel they could do someone else's better. You could well have observed that there is never any shortage of ideas in an organisation of what needs to be improved or put right, but it is always in someone else's patch, never one's own. The thalamocortical attention system is, perhaps, not designed to focus on self. For that, we humans have to employ our more highly evolved centres.

Other subcortical structures can also have an important affect on attention. We have all experienced those nagging thoughts that won't go away despite our earnest efforts. These are often associated with a state of anxiety, and our limbic nuclei keep pushing them to the forefront, aided and abetted by the hypothalamus stirring up the autonomic nervous system. Then, suddenly, something occurs which rivets our attention and all those nagging worries disappear, for a while. Emotion can be an important factor in any external event which attracts our attention, like bumping into a close friend or witnessing an accident. Evolution may well have devised our attention system to respond with priority to events which evoke emotion because survival could depend on decisive action rather than spending time debating among a number of options. If, for any reason, the attention system is not working properly, the individual can become confused by competing thought processes, and it has been postulated that a defect of this sort is responsible for some of the symptoms of schizophrenia[4].

There are skills we develop which do not require conscious attention because regular practise has enabled the basal ganglia to take over control from the neocortex. Many years ago when I was learning to drive, an indulgent colleague told me that driving was as straightforward as walking, which I reacted to with disbelief. And yet she was right, or almost. Most experienced drivers would agree that this quite complex activity can be undertaken with little attention. Automatic processes are involved with all highly practised skills, whether playing tennis or playing the piano, and if you have to pay a lot of attention to what you are doing you are probably not very good at it. High levels of training involving motor skills means that the neocortex does not have to focus attention on those activities. At other times failure to pay attention can result in slip-ups, or at least the fear of them. Did I lock the door as I left the house, did I switch off all the appliances and set the burglar alarm? Our attentional system weaves in and out of our daily activities, but there seems little doubt that if you want to remember an action or an event clearly, you have to pay attention. The hippocampus will only carry out its encoding operations if conscious aware-ness is present, and quite often it will require repeated or dramatic exposure to a subject in order to achieve secure declarative memory.

If we try and look at attention as it applies to populations we find our-selves faced with a difficulty, because we can never be certain what state of attention other people are in. They may give the impression they are attend-ing fully to what is going on, but in reality their thoughts may be miles away. Nonetheless, it is a virtual certainty that there will be a wide variation in attentional capacity between individuals. Professional golfers talk about the importance of concentration when they are under pressure in an import-ant tournament, especially in a finely graded task like putting. How many of us would claim to be able to give the undivided attention to the ball that they seem to do? The ability to concentrate and to become absorbed in a task is an enviable trait and one that I have often wished was more highly developed as far as my own mind was concerned, but a compensating thought is that I have probably been more adept than some at spotting predators creeping up from behind! We can conclude that the role of attention in thought is an important one because it plays a large part in determining what we think about, and how long we think about it.

Perception

This is another one of those terms where there is considerable overlap in common usage with another word used to describe mental events – *sensation*. Any attempt to differentiate between them is bound to tread on controversial ground, and all I can do is indicate the sense in which I intend to use them. Perception is always related to an external object or event, and it arises because we perceive something with our senses. The act of perception inevitably results in a sensation, which is the mind's interpretation of what we are perceiving. Of course, sensations can arise without any external stimuli, such as a sensation of pain or a sensation of wellbeing. We can also talk of *feeling* pain and a feeling of wellbeing. As a working convention, it can be assumed that there is a continuum between perception, sensation and feeling, with considerable overlap between them and influence of one on another, so that they are in a state of dynamic equilibrium. I hope this will become obvious in a moment with the examples I use. The defining principle of perception is that it involves interpretation of a phenomenon external to the self, though what we perceive is invariable coloured by sensation and feeling.

Any discourse on perception will vary with the background of the person examining the subject. A philosopher may well focus on intentionality, a neuroscientist on the complexities of neural processing, and a psychologist on the way we see depth, movement and form. All we need to do for our examination of thought is to acknowledge that many of the things we think about are associated with what we perceive. The senses through which we pick up our external inputs are most commonly visual or auditory, and we end up with an image which is processed in conjunction with elements of the thinking process that reside within the individual brain – sensation, feeling, memory, language, cognition. Because the way in which these variables combine will vary from person to person, we probably all perceive things slightly differently, especially if there are differences in the way the signals reach us, so that chaos theory can get to work. Let's try and clarify

the position with a specific example, where there are elements which introduce a certain amount of population variability into the perception.

   We are looking at a painting by Renoir in an art gallery. Although the
painting is stationary on the wall, the first remarkable thing is that we can
only see it because our eyes are moving all the time, picking up signals
which are later interpreted by the visual cortex as colours, lines, and shapes;
a process so complex that it involves neurons in nearly half the surface area
of the cerebral cortex. There are numerous accounts (e.g. Crick, Zeki,
Blakemore) of the amazingly intricate way neurons link up in this system,
and which parts of the visual cortex handle which signals, but there is as yet
no real understanding of how the brain binds all the elements together to
give us the effortless, holistic picture that we are consciously aware of.
Computational approaches have been tried, like the much admired early
work of David Marr[5], but many of the brain's visual secrets have still to be
unlocked. Even when we understand much better how the brain manages
the binding problem, we can never know whether we all see exactly the
same thing. It would be a wonder if we did with the potential for the
'butterfly effect' in that massive amount of neuronal circuitry. However, we
know there is sufficient fidelity in our visual processes for us to agree about
the main aspects of the painting: the number of people, their postures and
their dress. But that is just the start of the thought process, because from
then on all the other folk psychology factors come into play.

   The amount of conscious attention the painting gets will depend on your
interest in Renoir and art in general. Some people will stand before it for an
age, others will give it a mere glance. Your knowledge and memory will
give you some concept of what a masterpiece should be, and you may spend
time analysing it and savouring the emotional satisfaction it gives you. On
the other hand it may leave you cold, and you will quickly pass on. You
could even find it disturbing if it reminds you of some unpleasant experience in your past. The mere act of perception, then, is coloured by all sorts
of overtones, and those overtones are likely to be greater with a work of art
than, say, a perfectly ordinary chair. The differences between us are
amplified by the complexity of what we are looking at, or what we are
hearing, and the time we have to absorb it. In addition, we are consciously
aware of only part of what we perceive, and the position in which the
spotlight of attention rests will vary from person to person. If this is true
with a static work of art, just imagine the scope for variation in a moving
scene in which you are a participant and playing a role which is unique in
the sense that no one else is doing exactly the same thing as you, and in
which more than one sense is involved. The various channels for vision,
hearing and touch all interact with one another, and the aggregate sensation

which comes to the fore and is consciously registered is exclusively yours. No one else will have that same sensation, and in assessing another mind you have to make a crude assessment of what sensations it might be experiencing from the observable evidence. Needless to say, we mostly get it wrong.

If there are differences between individuals within the same culture in what they perceive, think of the gulf that can arise between cultures, say, between a *Guardian* reader and a *Daily Telegraph* reader! What is the taste of raw fish? We would receive very different answers from Japanese and British tasters as a result of cultural upbringing. Of course, it is always possible to modify perceptions, a fact I can heartily testify to as a lover of *sashimi*, and as one who once found it difficult to believe that the Japanese actually preferred their own food to Western dishes. Many of us can remember when we first tasted red wine, and thought what foul, astringent tasting stuff it was; immediately making a beeline for the Niersteiner. It requires persistence and dedication to develop real taste. Whenever value judgements have to be made, our lives are a history of changing perceptions as we become exposed to different stimuli over extended periods. If something goes tragically wrong with our brain it becomes obvious how perceptions can become distorted, as we have seen from some of the examples in Chapter 1. Differences between extremes are obvious, but what about all those fine gradations that appear as subtle physiological changes take place in our brains? It is here that our population distribution game and the bell-shaped curve help us to visualise the spread of possibilities.

There are many simple tests that psychologists have carried out to assess visual perception, some involving two-dimensional figures which are open to more than one interpretation, others using flashing lights which can be fused into one by the human visual mechanism. These provide valuable insight into the basic psychology of vision, showing how errors and illusions occur, but they do not discriminate to any great extent between the perceptual characteristics of individuals. In any case we have to define whether we are interested in perception in its primary guise, untrammelled by other interacting processes of thought, or perception as it lies after it has been fully digested mentally, and subjected to all the things that memory and emotion can do to it. I would suggest it is the latter which is of more interest in our daily lives. The fact that it is very difficult to carry out meaningful studies does not prevent us developing imaginary scenarios of ways in which this might be done. For instance, we could envisage stopping all solo car drivers on a motorway and asking them what they perceived between the census point and the previous junction. In this imaginary experiment we can ignore the traffic snarl-up and the fury it would cause. If we were able to conduct such a survey, how much common ground do you think we would find? Almost none? All right, so you think the conditions of this experiment are insufficiently standardised, because the drivers would be in different cars, travelling at different speeds in different lanes, and listening to different channels on the radio. Instead, should we go for the audience at Glyndebourne after the first act of Harrison Birtwistle's *The Second Mrs Kong*, rather than allowing them to drink champagne on the lawn during the interval? I suppose we would find rather less consistency here than in the Wagner audience we considered in Chapter 2. Perhaps a better bet might be a group of Chelsea supporters after their soccer team had lost at home. On the other hand, perhaps not. What about sampling viewers of a party-political broadcast on television? You can see the problem in measuring and categorising perceptions in real-life situations.

The mental background against which we view any event has an enormous impact on our final perception – the one we become consciously aware of. With no two people having the same background experience or neural architecture it is a nigh on impossible task to get any direct bearing on relative perceptual states because of the number of variables and their subjective nature. We have to revert to a secondary indicator. This is where *feelings* help us to get our bearings and decide on our actions. It is the difference between trying to interpret a long, verbose review of a newly released CD recording where we end up not knowing what the reviewer really thinks, and the enlightenment we could gain from a simple rating – excellent, good, average, poor. Think of the power of the Michelin Guide with its star rating of restaurants, compared with all the other waffly guides. This star-grading role of feeling is very much in line with what Antonio Damasio finds absent in his patients with damage to their prefrontal cortex. If your prefrontal cortex–limbic–autonomic circuits are not operating properly you have difficulty in deciding on your best future interests, because it is only the feelings that emerge which have the power to crunch the myriad of interactions and guide you to an appropriate decision. Of course, powers of rationality can and are brought to bear in determining any outcome, but their contribution depends on how well they are in balance with your emotional state and whether you allow them the power of arbitration. Perhaps the most highly developed sense of perception conceivable is to be able to see one's own interaction with a complex stimulus in a more or less objective light, something Thomas Nagel has called 'The View From Nowhere'[6]. Perception, as we are defining it, does not allow us to achieve that, but rationality can help, as we shall see later.

The conclusion I would like to reach from this brief examination of perception is that, in day-to-day life, perceptions become modified by a mixture of sensations, thoughts and feelings which arise both in the neocortex and the subcortex. The domain of thought is the neocortex, which is often regarded as the rational engine of the human brain. But there is never enough information processed by our neocortex to demonstrate with logical certainty that we have got it right on any subject matter resident in our thoughts. We have to refer to our beliefs which are bolstered by the emotional circuits of the subcortex. The outcome of this state of affairs is that a large percentage of the population will disagree with any assessment we make of the facts. The potential for difference can be difficult to detect if we are concerned with simple objects and simple perceptual tasks, such as identifying a chair. But if we move on to a more sophisticated evaluation of chairs we know that some people will prefer antique chairs and some ultra-modern chairs, and will respond to them in a different manner. This subjective response will have a lot to do with the value system of the individual and the emotional response it evokes in subcortical structures. There is no right or wrong but there can be a population reference point.

The standards by which judgements are evaluated are largely determined by the emergent-algorithm of culture and population. Let's take a certain kind of modern art where bricks are piled up in a gallery or a cow is preserved in formaldehyde solution. There is a subculture in the artistic community which ascribes a value to these exhibits and which largely ignores the derision of outsiders. Who is right – the in-crowd or the outsiders? We can place our bets but we cannot be sure of the answer until the emergent-algorithm of opinion in society has run its course, and that may take many years. If we were to take a population survey we might find there is a clear decision against this new form of art having any intrinsic merit but, historically we might have found that true for most new artistic departures. We can only wait and see and, of course, try and influence the outcome.

Memory

We considered some psychological categories of memory in Chapter 1. Here, I am not so much concerned with categorisation as what happens with memory during our conscious thought processes. *Working* and *declarative* memory are clearly important because they are the means by which we keep track of what is happening from moment to moment and how we can relate that to conscious recall of earlier memories. One point of crucial importance is the fidelity of memory. There is plenty of evidence that distortion of memory occurs quite frequently by the introduction of unwarranted inferences or through confabulation. Whether memories are accurate or not, they can obviously have a large impact on our perceptions, because what we perceive can be modulated by our memories and the emotions they generate.

Work with *split-brain* patients has shown that there are differences in the way the left and right hemispheres of the brain cope with memory. You will remember that these patients are people who have undergone a surgical operation to have their corpus callosum severed so that there is no direct connection between the left and right hemispheres. This allows the right and left sides of the brain to be tested separately. Such studies suggest that the left brain is much more adept at making inferences and creating interpretations of events than the right brain, which tends to stick to events as they were. Of course, in these patients, the right brain is not able to report its recollections verbally because language capability resides in the left brain, with which it has lost its connection. We have to regard such evidence as indicative and provisional but, at the moment, it is all we have. But when we think back in a fanciful manner to left-brained Frankie and right-brained Johnnie (Chapter 1) we might not be surprised to find that it is Frankie who is the great spinner of colourful stories and dour old Johnnie who tends to be regarded as a bit pedestrian in the way he sees things. No imagination, they say, but utterly reliable!

In a large organisation the way we remember things is often a very practical issue. There seems little doubt that some people's memories are better and more reliable than others. If this weren't the case there would not be much point in a Master Mind competition on television, even though its title is a bit misleading. Semantic Memory Mind might be more accurate but, perhaps, not quite so appealing. In a discussion with a colleague about what was said at a meeting, we are dealing with a combination of episodic and semantic memory, and it is often difficult to decide who has the most accurate memory of events and facts. Memory will be affected by differences in attention and perception at the time of the event, as well as nuances in interpreting language and any emotional overtones it might have carried. There is bound to be some subjective distortion in both memories and it is very common that temporal sequences in meetings get confused so that meanings get altered by memory of chronology. That is why a good secretary taking notes is invaluable. Where no record has been kept we would have to resort to a statistical procedure involving everyone at the meeting to get as near to the truth as possible. Our own memory serves our purpose as an individual organism and guides us in our thoughts and subsequent actions, but we should not deceive ourselves that we have precisely the same memory of a common experience as anyone else. In the end we have to rely on our own resources and the community in which we live will make its decision about our relative performance.

How are all these memories laid down and where, and how do we recall them? No one has much idea. There is evidence that synaptic changes are associated with long-term declarative memory, especially in the hippocampal complex, but that is only part of the story. Large areas of the neocortex are certainly involved, and different parts will be associated with different memories. A visual memory will activate regions in the visual cortex and linguistic memory will involve the language areas in the left brain. The problem of *where* is likely to be easier to solve than *how*. There is almost certainly no permanent, fixed record of everything we remember in the manner of a videotape recording or a computer disk, because the record shows that many memories are lost, changed or replaced over time. It seems likely that memories are linked to neuronal maps. These may be massive interlocking circuits of neurons involving many parts of the brain. How they are activated and memories retrieved poses an even thornier problem, but there is no doubt the system acts fast.

A little incident between Frankie and Johnnie will be illustrative. They are in the middle of a deep conversation and Johnnie suddenly says to Frankie, 'there's a spider on your arm'. During the next 300 milliseconds there is a sequence of events in Frankie's brain which can be illustrated schematically by employing the best evidence there is of where things might be happening:

- Auditory signal – thalamus; sensory cortex – Frankie hears
- Attention – thalamic system – her thoughts desert the conversation
- Procedural memory – linguistic areas, left sensory cortex – knows meaning of 'spider' and 'arm'
- Working memory – prefrontal cortex – retention of sentence milliseconds after completion
- Episodic memory – hippocampal system – recalls personal spider experience
- Motor activity – frontal cortex – head and eyes turn
- Perception – thalamus; sensory cortex – image of spider
- Semantic memory – hippocampal system – image and memory coincide confirming presence of spider
- Emotional memory – limbic system – can't stand spiders
- Violent brushing action – motor cortex; basal ganglia; cerebellum – spider knocked off arm

- Emotional reaction – limbic system; hypothalamus – adrenergic surge; increase in heart rate, muscle tremor, etc
- Episodic memory – hippocampal system – incident recorded. Frankie wonders why Johnnie didn't remove the spider for her!

Even in the simplest events that confront us some form of memory is involved, and yet we have no real idea how memories are encoded in the brain. Our perceptions 'play back' on our earlier experiences, because it is only if we have had earlier experiences that we can add meaning to what we perceive. This even applies to the process of vision, because unless the brain has been trained to respond to visual signals in the early years of its development, it cannot interpret them. In one sense, then, the brain remembers how to see. Is it any wonder then that there are such vast differences between each of us when we have all had such different formative experiences?

Language

There is probably nothing that more characterises the human species than language. Every human society, no matter how primitive, has the capacity for language, and no other species has shown anything resembling human linguistic ability. It must surely be a central reason for the evolutionary success of mankind, because it has allowed learning to be passed on from one generation to the next, at first by word of mouth and then by written texts. But is it language which allows us to think, or does it result from the way we think? This is a matter of considerable controversy and one it is not easy to resolve because it revolves around evolutionary arguments. Unfortunately, there is no fossil record for language and its development.

Derek Bickerton has emphasised the importance of language as a representational system, rather than as a means of communication, although it is clearly both[7]. He maintains that it was language which gave us our ability to work on problems that do not immediately confront us, something he has described as 'off-line' thinking. You may recall we used the expression 'off-line' in regard to 'off-line simulation' when discussing the ability to work out what was going on in someone else's mind. The evidence suggests that other species can only think 'on-line', that is their minds are only able to process the events of the immediate moment. They obviously have memories laid down from their own personal experience or they would not be able to recognise a potential source of food, a threat of danger, or decide what action to take. But it seems unlikely that they sit down and meditate about such matters. Language is certainly not the only representational system, and it is possible that other species could place their reliance on, say, visual imagery to aid thinking, but evidence is lacking for any 'off-line' capability. Bickerton has noted that although apes have manual dexterity and have produced abstract paintings, no chimpanzee has yet been found which can draw representationality *at all*. So much for the artistic capabilities of the species which shares 98.4% of our genes!

There seems little doubt that language is a considerable aid to our thinking processes even if the neurological basis of thought requires a representational system of a different kind, based, perhaps, on symbols or models that we employ subconsciously. Ray Jackendoff argues that thought is an unconscious process which only at a later stage takes the form of language or images[8]. He instances the experience of people who are totally bilingual, where it is not clear which language they are thinking in, and the experience that many of us have had of suddenly arriving at an intuitive conclusion without conscious deliberation. Other linguists/philosophers, like Steven Pinker[9] and Jerry Fodor[10], agree that natural language is not the vehicle for thought, that there must be some other process for thought; a 'mentalese'. I'm sure most of us can think of instances where we do not employ language for 'off-line' thinking. My own favourite example is planning the layout of a room in a new house, when furniture and fittings can be arranged in the mind's eye, complete with colour scheme. In such a situation we construct models in our mind which have little reliance on language. If, however, we turn to abstract arguments, it is very difficult to construct our models without the use of language, because the concepts we are using do not lend themselves to concrete imagery. In order to get our thoughts straight it is often necessary to set them down on paper and to play around with word order because our working memory cannot cope without a physical image of the sentence structure. The degree to which this is necessary will obviously vary from individual to individual.

Whether or not language evolved primarily as a representational system it is the discipline of communication which provides the acid test for many of us, because it is only then we begin to assemble our thoughts into a form which can be readily understood by others. The process of arranging our thoughts for a speech or a paper is one which requires considerable effort. During the course of our careers, many of us have dodged sitting down to write a paper setting out our thoughts in a way which would make them clear to everybody. I certainly have to plead guilty. It is an arduous and time consuming chore and there are many other things to be done which require dynamic action, rather than scribbling at a desk. Now that I am retired and have all the time in the world, things are rather different. I can afford to spend time staring at the computer screen or reading relevant material until ideas emerge. The comforting experience is that, if you do make the effort, concepts form where previously there was a vacuum. Language may have a Chomskyan tree-like deep structure, but there is no doubt in my own experience that one thought is contingent upon another in serial fashion, and until I get the first one down I have no idea what the second and third are going to be, let alone the fourth and fifth. I do not believe I can be unique in this, but once again we would need a properly constructed population study to find out to what extent linguistic constructions require a prompt from the previous thought, and whether a visual trigger is necessary.

We really have no option but to use language to communicate and this therefore appears to be its essential purpose and, presumably, the main reason for its evolution. But, it is also valuable to consider it as a repre- sentational system because we can then ask, 'What does language represent and how faithfully?' The fact is that language can only capture a mere fraction of anything we experience, because its serial nature does not facilitate descriptions of complex parallel events. We can illustrate the problem with a football match and an attempt to describe accurately the movement of all 22 players on the field. Because football has an outcome associated with the position of the ball, we normally concentrate on what is happening to the ball, and largely ignore the rest of the field. Language can cope with following the trajectory of one ball, but if there were three balls and we constructed the rules of the game so that we had to follow the aggregate paths of three balls it would make the task of description nigh on impossible. But, describing a game of football with three or more balls would be chickenfeed compared with describing parallel activity in the brain, with its millions of different circuits firing away simultaneously. When we use language we are looking for events which can be described in serial fashion; searching for a verbal picture of the way the emergent- algorithm manifests itself. The whole process of writing about history is a search for threads of this sort; threads which can be identified as having a significant impact on events. That is, of course, why history can be written in so many different ways.

Although language has its limitations in representing our thoughts and communicating them accurately to others, it does allow us to share concepts through shared memories. If I say our friend Renoir was an impressionist, it immediately means something to you. From this you can deduce that he probably lived in France at the turn of the century and knew a chap called Monet, who also painted in a certain style. The meaning of words and the relationship language establishes between them is an invaluable aid to thought. Whether or not language is necessary for the fundamental process of thought, it is certainly necessary to catalyse the process in many instances. For my own purposes it is also preferable for the language to be written down so that I can see it. Perhaps this is associated with a deficiency in my own short-term language memory, and once again there will be a spread of capabilities within the population. It was said of Bertrand Russell that he hardly ever corrected anything that he had written down, and yet in *The Language Instinct* Steven Pinker is adamant that good writing requires extensive revision. This is of great comfort to me, but I doubt whether Bertrand Russell would have been flattered. In truth, there will be great variation within the population, so that some people will be able to compose in their heads, others will struggle on paper. What it does not necessarily throw any light on is the quality of the final product.

Much of the structure of language, its syntax and grammar, appears to be built into the innate capacities of the human brain. We do not teach our children grammar. Many of us are unaware of the formal rules of grammar and it has been shown that children reared by parents speaking an un-grammatical pidgin language will soon turn it into a grammatical Creole language. The same applies to deaf children learning a sign language, where their parents have been unable to impart any grammar – they develop their own grammar. A basic ability to learn language seems to be genetically programmed into us, and the finer points of the language we learn as young children depend on the environment in which we find ourselves. At a funda-mental level of analysis all natural languages have a similar structure and conform to a *universal grammar* for syntactic structure, though some will depend on word order more than others and some place more emphasis on case markers. The essential point about language as it relates to thought is that it gives us a common discipline to relate concepts to one another, so that we can convey the essence of our thoughts to another person. The skill with which we can construct our sentences will determine how the other person reacts to what we say or write, and in normal social intercourse it is understandable that great premium is placed on such skill. If you happen to be a specialised mathematician, an organic chemist, or a composer of music, the representational system you will depend on will not be ordinary language, and your abilities may be judged as outstanding even if you are incoherent in verbal expression. For most of us in a working environment, though, it has to be accepted that ordinary language is the means by which we express ourselves and it will, to a large extent, determine how our mental abilities are judged. In making this judgement, however, we should not be too hasty because there may be something much deeper lying behind the coarse expressions that language allows us to make. Some researchers in the field of cognitive neuroscience believe that much thought is based on modelling in the mind, independently of language, and that there is significant involvement of the right hemisphere in developing these models.

Emotion

A good deal has already been said about emotion and feelings in the last chapter, and we now have to consider briefly how emotion can impact on and colour our thoughts. Everything we think about is pervaded by emotion to some degree, because the very fact that we are paying attention to a subject means that limbic circuits in the subcortex are active. With most 'attentional states' it will be possible to detect physiological changes affecting respiration, heart rate and peripheral blood flow which result from activation of the autonomic nervous system. The subject uppermost in our thoughts could be one which gives us a sense of satisfaction, a feeling of unease, a sensation of pleasure, or a sensation of dread. The list of possibilities is a long one. How often can we say we feel nothing at all? Each of us can readily detect, with the help of a little introspection, how our feelings relate to particular thoughts. But, it is also true that there is considerable variation in the level at which individuals react emotionally to their thoughts. Some react with observable emotion to everything, and others hardly seem to react emotionally at all. Lying below the external display are the feelings which will be obvious to the individual concerned but may well be entirely masked from an outside observer. It is clearly a difficult subject on which to get an objective handle, but personality traits can give us a clue. We could, for instance, differentiate between the behavioural extremes of obsessive–compulsive neurosis and zombie-like casualness, or between people with self-reliant personalities and those with dependent personalities. But, for the most part, we are concerned with the middle ground of the population distribution curve, and it is here we find a lot of difficulty in discriminating between individuals.

When we interact with other people it is helpful to know something about their emotional state, and the effect that it is likely to have on their thought processes, especially if we want something from them. It is a judgement that can be remarkably difficult to make. We might also want the other person to know how we feel, although find it impossible to convey the information in a way which is meaningful to them. Normal language is pathetically inadequate to describe with precision the complex mix of neuronal events which determine our emotional flux. In the last chapter I introduced a *default model*, which assumed that feelings could be the determining factor in our actions, and that those feelings could be captured by the effect they have on the activity of our autonomic nervous system. This autonomic indicator is a measure of our body's reaction to nervous activity on a scale of 1 to 7, from the negative depths of 1 to the positive highs of 7, with 4 representing our normalised state of comfortable equilibrium. We each have to calibrate ourselves on the basis of our own life's experience, so there can be no normalised calibration for the population as a whole. There is 'something-it-is-like' for each of us to feel in an emotionally neutral state, neither 'up' nor 'down', and in which, ideally, we should do most of our thinking if it is to suffer minimal interference from emotional effects, and when we are likely to be in our most rational frame of mind. Whether this neutral state is one we can equate with anyone else's neutral state is a question we cannot answer, but that is not the important point. The thing we want to know is whether our feelings are stable, or are fluctuating upwards or downwards. Is a particular thought or experience trending towards a more positive state or trending towards the negative (remembering that we are using this autonomic marker as an indication of our feelings)?

Just imagine, for the moment, that you have a barometer attached to your forehead which is not measuring atmospheric pressure but is indicating your state of euphoria or depression. When you are on an emotional high it moves above 4, and when you are down in the dumps the needle swings down below 4. The extent to which it moves will depend on how great your fluctuations in mood happen to be. You may not like your partner or friend to see the swing that occurs in reaction to something they say or do, but just think how informative it would be to them. If we really could gauge the reactions of others with this sort of precision it could save a lot of unnecessary heartache, assuming that we care about the reaction of the other person. All this is rather fanciful, but the only point I would like to make is that our thought processes are bound to be affected by these swings in mood, especially if we are largely unaware of the effects they can have. If we can consciously register that our feelings have changed in a significant way by an event or by something someone has said, then we are in a position to make due allowance for that change in applying any rational thought process. There is very little evidence about how people do assess their moods when evaluating situations, but I would hazard a guess that the question is hardly ever posed during normal operation of 90% of minds.

There are obviously many different factors which affect the way we feel. The satiation we gain from eating a good meal is qualitatively dissimilar from the orgasmic pleasure of a sexual experience or the sense of achievement from a successful endeavour. At the other end of the spectrum, the despondency felt at being let down by a friend is quite different to the sadness experienced through bereavement or the worry of an organic illness. But, what can be said with a large element of confidence is that the limbic system is involved in all these reactions, particularly the amygdala, and the hypothalamus with its connections to the autonomic nervous system. There are many tunes that can be played on a system as complex as this but, I predict, a population study would indicate that quite typical markers are associated with positive and negative states for most individuals, which they normally don't analyse but could easily do so if trained. We all seek circumstances which make us comfortable with ourselves, and the extremes of behaviour we see in society may well be associated with the quest of people to achieve this sense of internal comfort. The ideal for enhancing our higher mental processes is that we should be able to step outside these states and recognise them for what they are. This would lead to enhanced rationality and a reduction in aberrant behaviour.

Cognition

Having examined the basic components essential to everyone's thought processes, who would deny that some are deeper thinkers than others; that some have the ability to develop and extend thoughts in a way not open to the majority? Such ability may be ascribed to intellectual powers, to creative mental processes, to the rationality of a logical mind, or like cognitive attributes. What is going on when we start to think on a higher plane, and is there any possibility of developing a model of what is happening? Remember, we are trying to understand how other minds might differ from our own, and to do that it is helpful to have some sort of framework, even if it's a bit rickety. We can always repair and strengthen it later on. From the evidence we have looked at to date I think there is a possibility of developing a useful model, but to do that I need to pull the pieces of evidence together, and for that it is better to start another chapter.

Chapter 5

The Cognitive Element of Thought

Language of Thought

We have seen that there are many elements of the mind which impact on the nature of thought, but this does not throw much light on the fundamental structures underlying the more elevated cerebral processes. I intend to consider such processes under the general heading of *cognition* to indicate that we are considering secondary levels of thought where knowledge and experience are processed to produce a synthesis, often on an extended 'off-line' basis. We have little idea which systems in the neocortex are employed during our moments of cognitive contemplation, but the areas of the left hemisphere involved with language must be strong candidates. Jerry Fodor maintains that the mind employs a coded, computational process for thought, though it does not involve the language we speak. After all, a child has to think in some way in order to learn a language, which cannot realistically be the language itself. Many supporters of artificial intelligence believe the brain is best viewed as a computational device employing a coded representational system which acts in a serial manner like a language, but others believe it can be more accurately regarded as employing parallel systems which rely on the adjustment of vectorial values with no need for a programmed language[1]. We are not in a position to decide where the truth lies between these or any other points of view, but the evidence does indicate, beyond any reasonable doubt, that language greatly enhances the process of thought. Whatever the neuronal processes underlying thought may be, they need to emerge as language for us to make real progress.

Ray Jackendoff has urged that thought should be considered as an unconscious process, based on a hidden conceptual grammar that eventually emerges as a conscious event which can be translated into language. If we follow his advocacy we have to ask ourselves what the nature of this unconscious process could be. There are a number of neuroscientists and philosophers who have written about ideas which may be relevant, including Gerald Edelman, Bernard Baars, Daniel Dennett, and Susan Greenfield. Their terminology varies but their concepts all centre around the presence of competing neuronal maps throughout the global workspace of the cerebral cortex, with one of these maps eventually becoming dominant. The way that Susan Greenfield describes her ideas is particularly helpful in forming an image[2]. She employs the analogy of raindrops falling into a puddle and causing multiple ripples on the surface of the water. These ripples interfere with one another, and it becomes a question of whether they compete and disrupt each other or coalesce into one dominant ripple. When neuronal maps in the brain combine to form the equivalent of a dominant ripple, they provide the basis of consciousness. She sees this as the process of consciousness itself, as do some of her neuroscientific colleagues. Bernard Baars[3], for instance, employs the model of a *Global Workspace* in the brain where neuronal networks interact to produce a 'dominant gestalt', which is selected for conscious awareness through the agency of the thalamus and its links with the neocortex. Greenfield also uses the term 'gestalt' to describe the neuronal network which wins the competition for a place in consciousness. Edelman tends to prefer 'map' as his central term and refers to 'multiple re-entrant maps with global mappings'. Dennet refers to competition between 'multiple drafts'. These differences in terminology can cause a certain amount of confusion, but they all attempt to describe a scene where many neuronal firing patterns are competing with each other below the level of consciousness. It is only when the winner produces a conscious experience that we become aware of a thought.

The difficulty of providing evidence to support any of these concepts will be readily apparent, and at the moment we remain in the realm of theory as to the nature of the process leading to conscious thought. But the idea of competing neuronal maps which can result in a dominant gestalt does give us a way of considering how thought processes may vary between individuals. No one has any idea how many neuronal maps may be active in our brain at any one time, but it is fair to suppose there will be many hundreds, depending on our state of activity. Vital functions in the body have to be maintained and homeostasis preserved by lower centres in the brain at the same time as sensory and motor centres control actions which enable us to cope with our environment at a subconscious level. We can all entertain deep thoughts while driving our cars, for instance, without too much detriment to the performance of either task, and we have no difficulty in washing our various bodily parts in the shower without thinking about the actions we have to perform in order to achieve sparkling cleanliness. The more we concentrate on the thought at hand, the less we will be aware of other sensory stimuli around us and our response to them. Neuronal maps will be emerging and decaying without most of them reaching conscious awareness, and it is only when one of them flips into the conscious spotlight that we become aware of it and translate it into language, images, or emotion. The possibilities can be illustrated by returning to our population distribution game.

Population Variation

If we mentally scan through all the people we know, or have known, to assess their mental characteristics when asked to make a choice or decide on a course of action, it is likely that we will be able to identify those who have difficulty in making up their mind and have a tendency to keep changing it. At the other end of the spectrum will be those who are decisive and highly focussed when challenged by some task, with an enviable ability to concentrate on and resolve the matter in hand. Susan Greenfield sees consciousness as a continuum, with the wandering consciousness in a young baby developing into the more focussed adult consciousness as the child grows up. Levels of consciousness also vary within each of us as individuals as we pass from a dreamy, half-awake state into a state of full arousal. Whether we can accept this analysis depends on how we define consciousness, but there can be little doubt that there are identifiable differences in mental processes involving thought patterns that can be associated with conscious states. Just as there is an axis between adult and child and between being half asleep and fully aroused, so there is likely to be an axis between the population extremities of minds on the bell-shaped distribution curve, with some people constantly shifting from one thought to another, and others with the ability to concentrate intently on a single issue. The extremes could be caricatured by 'the butterfly mind' versus 'the absent-minded professor' who often gets lost in thought. To illustrate the latter extreme we might take Beethoven or Shakespeare. Whatever the innate talent or intellect required to produce their supreme works of art, who can doubt that their brains had to focus intently on what they were doing for extended periods of time, to the exclusion of other thoughts. No multiplicity of neural maps here all competing with one another for attention, but one gigantic, global map gradually developing a particular line of thought. It might be viewed as a hierarchy of maps, with one map having established itself as the master plan and gradually absorbing subsidiary maps until the great work of art is finally achieved: co-operative team effort between maps being the order of the day rather than competitive elimination, so that in the end a huge edifice is built. Perhaps we are all capable of this, to a degree, but for some reason we do not have the motivation to persist; the emotional satisfaction is not there. It seems reasonable to assume that both Beethoven and Shakespeare derived a certain amount of pleasurable satisfaction from their labours, otherwise it is hardly likely they would have persisted with them. Emotional factors can certainly be involved in a less admirable form of extended thought, such as that exhibited by the single issue fanatics who find it difficult to disengage their thoughts from the issue which obsesses them.

At the other extreme, we might consider an Alzheimer's patient or someone suffering from schizophrenia, where there is great difficulty in focussing on any subject for more than a short span of time. There appear to be multiple, transient maps buzzing away all the time and an inability to form a dominant thought sequence which relates to the external world. Of course, different mechanisms in the brain can be involved in disrupting normal thought processes. In the Alzheimer's patient there are physical changes in neuronal structures and schizophrenia is associated with an imbalance in neurotransmitter profile. We all know that when we become agitated it is difficult to concentrate as well as we do normally, and that involves the influence of emotional centres in the subcortex. It is also apparent that minds capable of great and extended thought can go wrong, as happened with Schumann and Nietzsche, and it may be there is a fine balance between mental stability and creative thought.

Most of us occupy a mid-position on the spectrum, and in my own case I have already indicated my powers of concentration are not particularly good. If I had to analyse the eddies and currents in my own mind which make up the ebb and flow of thought, I would have to say there are numerous competing maps. I am sensitive to stimuli, both internal and external, and I can easily be distracted. If we were to plot a bell-shaped distribution curve of mental states ranging from a *coherent, single map* model to a *multiple, competing maps* model, I would probably find myself on the 'multiple' side of the mean. It is worth making this point because I would not like anyone to think I was making a value judgement about people or the nature of their thought processes. Whether conscious thoughts are held on to for long periods or disposed of quickly says nothing about levels of intellect or creativity, but it may be helpful to have awareness of this factor in forming a judgement about another mind and how it operates in comparison to our own. Most of us are going to be pretty similar on the neural map criterion, because 68% of us will fall within one standard deviation of the mean (however we decide to measure it). If you have got this far in this book it seems unlikely that you will be much towards the *competing, multiple maps* extreme of the curve, and if you had a *coherent, single map* tendency, with a purist scientific or philosophical bent, you would have probably given up in despair long ago. Even if, as a probable one standard deviation person, you think I am being a little fanciful, wait until you come upon a mind that is a total mystery to you, and reflect on the possibilities!

An Aside on the Power of Numbers

At this point I would like to correct any impression I may be giving that I believe it is possible to give a comprehensive account of human thought processes. In a rather simplistic way I think I can convey why the chances of doing this in the foreseeable future are virtually non-existent. The reason lies in the immense number of possibilities that can be generated by quite simple networks, let alone the staggeringly complex networks of the brain. If we imagine a 10×10 grid and we count the sides of the component squares we will find there are 220 sides. Each side can be viewed as representing a synapse, with the possibility of it being 'on' or 'off', i.e. firing or not firing. Even within this very simple arrangement there is the possibility of generating 2^{220} (or 10^{66}) different patterns. This is an immense number but it is trivial compared with the number of synaptic patterns that could be generated in a cubic millimetre of neocortex containing 100,000 neurons. These might generate 10^9 to 10^{10} synapses, so the possibilities become astronomical: in the order of $10^{1,000,000,000}$. In addition to this, synapses are not simple 'on/off' gates; they have plasticity affected by gene expression, protein synthesis, neuromodulators, neurotransmitters, and receptor profiles. Each neuron in the neocortex receives about 10,000 presynaptic connections and its transmitting axon ends up with synapses on another 10,000 neurons[4]. The axon transmits impulses from the receptive part to the transmitting part at rates up to approximately 100 per second, so this means that in 400 milliseconds it would be possible for all 10^{15} synapses in the cerebral cortex to be engaged, supposing they were linked in the right manner. It will gradually be possible to improve our knowledge and trace broad associations between brain function and neuronal activity, but the chances of ever identifying the precise neuronal correlate of a complex thought must be vanishingly small.

I have already mentioned several theories about how neuronal networks may generate activity in the mind. There are many others. Walter Freeman[5] believes that chaotic patterns are generated in the brain which only have meaning within the context of previously established, non-repeatable neuronal firing patterns. William Calvin[6] has put forward an intricate theory of neuronal connections which occur in triangular and hexagonal arrays and which recruit further arrays along the lines of Darwinian copying. The problem that confronts us is how to test any of these theories. With the unimaginably immense number of possibilities we have to say that the chances of doing so in any definitive manner are very slim. All we can realistically hope for is to identify an overall pattern of activity, something that chaos theory has labelled an *attractor*. An attractor is a stable pattern into which a chaotic system can settle. It describes the behaviour of the system, and it can change into a different pattern if circumstances change. The description of an attractor can only ever approximate to the real state of the system: the limitations imposed by the serial nature of linguistic description see to that. To illustrate the point, we might take an attack of influenza. The body is invaded by millions of viruses which replicate inside individual cells. Cytokines and antibodies are released to combat the invader. During the course of the infection we observe feverishness, prostration and headache in the patient. This can be described as the 'attractor state' of influenza which leads to a reliable medical diagnosis. However, if we were to try and describe the state of the patient cell by cell, RNA molecule by RNA molecule, glycoprotein by glycoprotein, we would soon be defeated. Similarly with the brain, we can only hope to find attractor states associated with thought which have a general correspondence to what is happening at the neuronal and subneuronal level.

An additional problem is that each of us has an individual, discrete personality, which might be described as the attractor state of our own central nervous system operating within the environment of our body's metabolism. Countless billions of molecular interactions are taking place from moment to moment, and the evidence suggests that the variations these produce between individuals are at least as significant as the similarities in the genetic template which guides our basic homeostatic processes. In the case of our neurons and their connections, we have variations built up by experiences during the course of our life histories, and these amplify any inherent differences in the repertoire of feelings and thought processes we are each aware of. Our sense of individual continuity and our sense of uniqueness is built on our memory of such experiences. Statistical techniques are probably the only avenue open to us to gain an insight into how other minds might operate in comparison to our own.

Qualitative Aspects of Thought

With these reservations we have to probe a little deeper into what the qualitative aspects of thought might be, and in doing so we cannot neglect the role of the emotional component of mind in determining what we think about. Why do people take an interest in Egyptology or wild mushrooms and spend a large part of their lives following up their favourite subject? Obviously, it must produce some kind of emotional satisfaction; the feelings generated are rewarding to the individual. It means that the dominant neural map and all its subsidiaries are linked to a circuit involving the prefrontal lobe–amygdala–hypothalamus–autonomic nervous system nexus, which Antonio Damasio has postulated is associated with feelings. This linkage is critical to the level at which we pursue thought since, as discussed in the last chapter, feelings are the one reliable indicator we have on what is or is not rewarding to the organism. Sometimes we have to pursue thoughts which are not particularly pleasurable or stimulating, like filling in a tax return. In these circumstances we often delay the evil day as long as we can. It would be interesting to see a distribution curve plotted between those who hate to fill in tax returns and those who love to. Predictably, it would take on the side profile of a slab of cheese, so the curve is not always bell-shaped!

If feelings determine the extent to which we pursue thought, we have to consider what the other limitations might be, and it is here we come to the most difficult and contentious part of our deliberations because we enter the world of intellect and creativity. Leaving intellect aside for the moment we can consider what makes up the *creative* world of a Charles Dickens or an Anthony Trollope; both highly imaginative and prolific on a narrative plane. Their talent was far removed from the world of abstract thought, where philosophers exert their abilities, but their capacity for inventing descriptive detail was superlative – Dickens in the sheer artistry of his language and Trollope in painting scenes so realistic that the reader is absorbed into the action of his novels. It is not their ability to do it just once; there is probably no such thing as a one work genius; but their ability to perform to order year after year at such an extraordinary level. We could just as well consider Wagner, who combined at least two extraordinary talents, but I do not want to make our deliberations any more contentious than they need be. We could construct our bell-shaped curve for creative literary potential, and at one extreme we would have to place Dickens and Trollope. Who at the other extreme? Well, if someone is illiterate they would not stand much chance of writing a novel, but in the case of people like myself, though having a reasonable degree of literacy, I would place them more than one standard deviation on the wrong side of the curve through having no imagination for descriptive detail. It is quite easy to observe in a working population that a talent for description and a talent for analysis call on quite different aspects of mind.

So, in the creative writer we have an ability for the mind to fabricate or recount experiences in glowing detail, fashioning words with greater or lesser facility. There seems little doubt that memory must play a significant part in the process, and it seems likely that the right sort of memory maps are crucial for the creative process. I do not have much first-hand experience of story-tellers but I would hazard a guess that they are as much influenced by internal stimuli as by external perceptions. In that sense their internal world may be fantasy driven, placing their egos and imagination in a dominant position opposite the external world. This is pure speculation and we would have to carry out a properly controlled population study to find out whether there is a real trend in this direction. There is, however, one observation I am pretty confident of. If we move away from the world of the story-teller novelist to that of the historian, economist, sociologist, or philosopher who tries to describe the world around us, there is not necessarily a correlation between their descriptive powers and their ability to assess the probability of where the truth lies. Writing ability can be shrouded in the mists of the individual ego, where rationality and its capacity to assign probability to belief do not loom large. With the novelist we do not have to worry about conflicting views, but as soon as someone starts writing about the world as it is or was, we have a judgement to make in the context of all the other evidence. If this evidence is contradictory, the judgement about what to believe or not to believe can be difficult, and it may be impossible to resolve the situation with any degree of confidence, though most of us will decide where we want to place our bets. Those with a strong tendency towards belief may stake their soul, others may decide on a somewhat smaller stake. In the end, the matter will be resolved by the emergent-algorithm of history.

Johnny never ceases to be amazed at the way Frankie recounts the events of her working day in glorious Technicolor, whereas his day is a blur of grey. Frankie often complains that he doesn't tell her anything of human interest about his office colleagues, whereas she provides all the spicy details. Johnny maintains that nothing much of interest ever happens, which Frankie finds hard to believe. The fact that they work in different departments in the same organisation suggests their environments are not too dissimilar, and it is their emotional interests which are stirred by different things. Johnnie's mind tends to float on a sea of issues, while Frankie is more absorbed in what people are up to. She even writes letters to her family and friends, which Johnnie wouldn't do in a thousand years. He wouldn't know what to say. Despite being well matched intellectually it is easy to see that they fall a standard deviation or two apart on the bell-shaped curve of creative narrative ability. This could be a left- brain versus right-brain issue, but we have no easy means of finding out. Even if they submitted to PET or MEG scans the simple mental tasks they could be set would not show up significant differences. Such variation almost certainly lies within the fine detail of their neural networks rather than in simple topographical maps of grey matter. Fortunately, Frankie and Johnnie are enlightened enough to be amused and entertained by their contrasting attitudes rather than to find them cause for serious contention. It certainly helps with division of labour when they have to do a turn at the golf club Christmas party. Frankie's the scriptwriter, Johnnie's the performer.

Intellectual pursuits would appear to require rather different mental capacities to creative literary invention. Although we have many tests for measuring intelligence, no one seems to be quite certain what it is, except the ability to perform in a certain manner in intelligence tests. We can all recognise high intelligence when we see it, though. It is associated with a person's powers of reasoning and understanding, particularly on an abstract plane. There are many intelligent people who are not intellectuals, the latter term being reserved for those who pursue learning in a systematic way, so that it becomes a way of life. Quite often they pursue their interests to the neglect of every-day matters, when they can become characterised as 'un-worldly'. The label of 'intellectual' can almost become a stigma in politics because it implies someone thinks too much for their own good and cannot handle the rough and tumble of interpersonal relationships. For our purposes, perhaps it will suffice to define intellectual ability as the capacity to process information in an extended manner combined with a formidable bank of usable knowledge stored in the memory. That knowledge may be highly specialised and of little value in the hurly burly of daily life, but it does say something about the cerebral cortex and its capacities, because that knowledge can be accessed readily and manipulated mentally in complex ways. What does that mean in terms of cerebral maps? They are almost certainly to a large extent in the cortex with circuits in the frontal lobes playing an important role. We do not know where memories are stored in the brain, or how access to them is obtained, but it seems likely that memory maps are formed by configurations of neurons and changes laid down at the synaptic level. Memory alone is not sufficient, though, because different memories have to be combined and sorted, and synthesised with new information to form novel concepts. If the ability to form novel concepts is absent then the level of intellectual capacity is likely to be low. Mnemonists cannot disguise themselves as intellectuals. Obviously, we are now into highly complex neuronal circuitry, and it will be aeons before neuroscience can determine what is happening, if indeed it is within the scope of human capabilities at all. One thing it should be possible to say about intellectuals is that they can concentrate. The neural maps we were talking about earlier tend to coalesce into one big, dominant global map. At least, we can assume this as a model for our discussion.

Where does this leave us? All I have suggested so far is that it is possible that the deeper and more sophisticated levels of cerebral activity require mental processes that rely on a series of interlocking neural maps which can combine in incremental steps to produce a substantial edifice of thought. This can be contrasted with lighter levels of cognitive activity, say a state of day-dreaming or a state of nervous agitation, when neural maps are transient and displace one another rapidly, so that thought tends to flit from one subject to another and never develops into a global or extended pattern. This model derives most directly from Susan Greenfield's theorising about consciousness, where she postulates that the actual size of a gestalt (neural map) corresponds directly to the degree of consciousness. The problem I have with this formulation is that, if there is a gradation in consciousness between child and adult, and between dreaming and full arousal, what does this mean for a comparison of consciousness levels within a given adult population? We can be pretty confident that the thought processes of attendees at a meeting differ widely, but if someone's mind is wandering and they are not concentrating on what the speaker is saying, can we maintain they are any less conscious than their neighbour? Of course, it depends how we define consciousness, but if the definition is confined narrowly to that process which translates neuronal activity into subjective experience, it would not seem possible to make such a distinction

If there is anything in the neural map model, extension of thought would seem to be a more promising avenue than consciousness because it is possible to envisage certain measurements being applied to thought patterns, and even if we are not in a position to carry out measurements we can apply guidelines and judgements to ourselves and others. For instance, we can now consider the role of language, since extended thought processes would seem to be impossible without language, whether or not the underlying processes of thought are conscious or unconscious. Once again I have to resort to analysing my own experience since I am not in the privileged position of being able to undertake a population study and, in any case, it would be very difficult to undertake one at the level required. I am quite clear that to extend my own ideas the stages of the process have to be set down in the form of written language, though, no doubt, the extent to which this applies to others will vary from individual to individual. One can think of the example of Mozart composing whole symphonies in his head in the language of musical notation, but I would guess most composers have to resort to pen and paper. Memory capacity in my case is simply inadequate to retain a fixed and reliable image of a particular stage in the thought process so that the next can be built on to it. I have no way of knowing whether I am around the mean of the population in this particular capacity, but it wouldn't surprise me if my ability to use in-built linguistic memory was somewhat worse than average. It is only if I take the trouble to set thoughts down that I can make real progress in conceptual thinking. Structural thinking is a different matter, as our friends Frankie and Johnnie demonstrate.

Johnnie has never felt the need to keep an updated diary in the way that Frankie does, because he is able to structure time in his own mind and maintain a clear memory of future commitments. He also has a well-developed spatial sense, and hardly ever loses his sense of direction. It is often a sense of wonder to him that Frankie has so little idea where they are when they have been walking or driving for a while. Frankie is something of an addict for the use of decision-trees in business planning, but Johnnie considers them a waste of time. He maintains it is possible to see the available options and to decide on the best path forward without using spurious quantitative techniques on paper. He cannot recall a time when a decision-tree ever added anything useful to deliberations. All possible paths forward are fraught with uncertainty and he finds it fairly easy to gauge where there are significant differences in the probabilities of expected outcomes. Frankie disagrees. She feels she has to get things written down before she can see the overall pattern sufficiently well to make an important decision. She often accuses Johnnie of not having thought things through sufficiently when he makes decisions, though she has to concede that things go right for him far more often then they go wrong. He certainly makes decisions much more quickly than she does and he thinks she can be a bit of a fusspot in setting down all the options. Johnnie is the first to concede, though, that if a detailed description of plans is required, Frankie is much better at producing an account that other people can follow easily. Once again we can speculate that right-brain/left-brain factors may be at work, but whether they are or not, there is no doubt that their brains work in markedly different ways. This even reaches down to what each of them remembers and doesn't remember. But, like Jack Spratt and his wife, they make a formidable pair in keeping life's platter clean.

Thought process, then, can be very different even between people who have a close relationship, and, generally, the only external clues we have about what they are thinking is through what they say. Although Ray Jackendoff reckons that the grammatical form of language probably gives some indications about the underlying structure of thought, this would only seem to apply if the representational system in question involves natural language. If we are thinking about a musical score or a chemical reaction,

the representational system we employ is quite different. We can communicate ideas in these spheres without resorting to the grammar of
language. Even when we resort to language there is a lot of uncertainty
around the edges of the way we express ourselves and the way what we say
is interpreted. Much depends on the background assumptions and experience of the speaker and the hearer and, indeed, John Searle[7] believes
Background is so important he uses it as a technical term with a capital B.
Much of the analysis of language by philosophers and linguists is on very
simple phrases and their variants, where meanings can be shown to depend
on context and the extent to which practices are shared. Being neither a
philosopher nor a linguist I will not advance further on this thorny ground
but simply observe that, if there can be confusion over simple sentences,
what chance for misunderstanding with large tracts like the one you're
reading now? I have often felt over the years that spoken or written language is much less precise than thought. How often have you felt that you
know what you want to say but you find difficulty in finding the words
which give true fidelity of expression to the thought? It has certainly
happened to me many times; and this despite the fact that natural language
provides an immense amount of flexibility. The problem may lie with its
serial nature and the limitation of expressing only one thought at a time,
whereas we can envisage multiple interactions in our minds.

Language is crucial to the way the *classical* school of artificial
intelligence (AI) views the workings of the mind. It bases its theories on
mental representations being derived through a structured and coded system
of symbols, such as we observe with language. The *connectionist* school of
AI adherents believe that the brain's processes are better represented by
networks which work in a highly parallel fashion and place little reliance on
symbolic algorithms. Is it possible that the brain uses a combination of
these, and perhaps other, systems because of its immense capacity? It is
understandable that philosophers and mathematicians often think in terms
of coded systems, because these are the tools of their trade, and if we could
examine their neural maps we might find evidence of left-brain dominance.
Skill with language obviously has an immensely influential role in human
society and has been vital for the advancement of the species because it
provides the ability to communicate through space and time. But we should
not undervalue the role of other cognitive qualities. Have you noticed there
are some people who are not particularly skilled at expressing themselves
but who exhibit eminent good sense and achieve outcomes they cannot
always articulate in an easily understood manner? The world of science
provides some good examples of this when papers are written in such a
turgid manner that the message becomes extremely obscure. The insight

they contain only becomes apparent to the world when a skilled interpreter intervenes. Is the nature of scientific insight concerned with language or more with networks which connect up in complex ways and throw up patterns of relationships not previously apparent to the world? My money would be on the latter.

Paul Churchland (Chapter 5, Reference 1) is unusual for a philosopher in that he tends to regard language as unimportant for thought. He believes that our cognitive processes rely on vector coding and vector to vector transformations in parallel networks. A vector is like a discrete setting on a variable volume control, and it is easy to envisage that synaptic connections of neurons are capable of arranging themselves to respond to signals at different levels. The combination of possibilities becomes enormous, even with a relatively small number of settings. It is easy to see this with the cones of the retina which basically respond to red, blue and green light. The gradations by which enormous numbers of cones respond to these three primary colours enables us to make fine discriminations in the colours of objects, and on top of that the brain undertakes computations so that we can recognise colours even when the light changes. All of our sensory systems employ vector coding of this sort, and they gave rise to thought in our early ancestors two million years ago when they were shaping stone tools for hunting and had not yet developed language. There seems little doubt that language is not necessary for all thought, but it becomes indispensable when we start intellectualising about abstract ideas and want to formulate them in a way that we can communicate to others. It may be that our descendants will one day invent a representational system that is much more effective in depicting complex parallel thoughts than the language we use today, and, indeed, that step may be necessary before we can properly understand the brain and its conscious activities.

Consciousness obviously plays an important role in our thoughts, since we need to consider how we become aware of what we are thinking about. We do not know the answer but it seems reasonably certain that our attentional system has an influential role and that subcortical structures are involved. So, all that fancy high-level intellectual and creative activity in the neocortex in some way depends on more primitive areas of the brain. It can be said that our attention system limits us to thinking about one thing at a time, which may be true in large measure, but it does not give us much of a clue about the nature of the thing a person may be thinking about at a particular moment. Supposing we could wire up the mind of a soprano performing on stage when she is singing a difficult aria. She has to be aware of the other performers, move to cued positions on the set, perform certain dramatic gestures, listen to the line of the music, find the right words, hit the right notes, and watch the conductor. She may well have programmed much of this activity into subconscious processes in her brain during rehearsals, but for everything she is doing there has to be appropriate neural activity. It is only when we ask, 'What is she conscious of?' at a given moment, that we come up against the limitations of thought in terms of the attentional system. There is presumably some rapid switching going on as the performance of our prima donna would not be possible if she had to encase her mind in a single neural gestalt. That might have been necessary when she was learning her lines and how to sing the music, but she cannot afford to be lost in thought when on stage. Rapid scanning of what is going on about her seems to be as absolute a requirement as remembering her own part, and some of that activity would appear to be at the edge of consciousness rather than due to discrete switching between neural maps. The fact that such performances are possible suggests that the thought we are conscious of at a given moment is just the tip of the iceberg of neural activity.

As impressive as the performance of an opera singer may be, our main concern is with thought processes and their evaluation in situations where rational decisions have to be made. In the next chapter we at last arrive at the heart of our deliberations.

Chapter 6

Thought and Rationality

Clarifying Rationality

In Chapter 2 I provided a definition for rationality: *the assignment of probability to belief in calculating outcomes or making judgements.* There are, of course, other possible definitions, and many philosophers would want to incorporate reference to deductive logic in any statement. Harold Brown[1] is a philosopher who has developed a model of rationality that moves away from logic and requires rational beliefs to be based on judgement. His definition has obvious similarities to my own, but he doesn't specify exactly how judgements are to be made. In my own case I am attaching central importance to an assessment of the balance of probabilities when considering beliefs. Although this may sound rather formalistic it is an approach which has to be adopted in many businesses as they make forecasts about the future: what are the chances of technical success with a new product, how likely is the achievement of sales and profits forecasts, how credible is the projected rate of return on a new investment? At first sight it may seem that this sort of judgement has little to do with every-day personal and family life but, in fact, we are constantly confronted by situations which require us to believe or not to believe in a right course of action: buying a house or car, taking out insurance, assessing the reliability of a friend or neighbour, trusting or not trusting our spouse. We often formulate our beliefs in such situations on the basis of feelings, but it may also be advisable to submit the evidence to scrutiny. There is nothing like an example to illustrate the point, and for this I will turn to Frankie and Johnnie.

Frankie is an enthusiast. You will remember she likes exciting experiences and is something of a sensation seeker. Johnnie, on the other hand, likes to avoid over-stimulation. Frankie is all for action and might be considered by some to be impulsive. Johnnie likes a quiet life. They are on holiday in Scotland and have hired a boat for the day on Loch Tay. As they set out from Kenmore to Killin they find they have a head-wind which makes the surface of the loch quite choppy and it takes them much longer than planned to get to Killin, in the process using rather more petrol than expected. Johnnie gets quite worried, but Frankie is unconcerned about getting back on time or the possibility of running out of fuel. She insists

105

they stay for lunch as planned while Johnnie is constantly looking at his
watch and contemplating getting stuck in the middle of the loch because
they have run out of fuel. He is rather ashamed of the feelings which cause
his concern and is conscious of the danger of spoiling their day out. In the
end he suppresses his concerns and decides to go along with Frankie's
time-table. They land back in Kenmore an hour late with a thimble-full of
petrol in the tank. Frankie had actually telephoned from Killin to say that
they would be late back and the boat-hirer was unconcerned. The day
ended happily.

We can see two different kinds of mind at work here. Thoughts about the
complications of the day don't even enter Frankie's mind as she finds herself on an emotional tide of enjoyment. Poor old Johnnie cannot help but
contemplate all the things that could possibly go wrong, and his concerns
are not helped by the effects of the prevailing wind in prolonging the
journey. He cannot avoid thinking about these things because that is the cast
of his mind, and the feelings his thoughts engender are not helpful in
making Frankie's day enjoyable. However, Johnnie is a rational man. He
realises there is only a small probability of his fears proving justified and he
decides to take the risk and ignore them. Fortunately they did not get stuck
in the middle of the loch through lack of fuel, which was the worst foreseeable outcome, and their deposit was not forfeited because of Frankie's
foresight in telephoning the boat-hirer. Once again their combination of
personalities had paid off. In other circumstances the outcome might have
been quite different, with the storm getting worse and resulting in a distressing experience, or Johnny pursuing his worst fears unnecessarily and
resulting in a rupture with Frankie. These fine balances are presented to all
of us day-in, day-out, and the way we handle them affects our lives. The
question is, do we just follow our feelings or does rational reflection help?

Although this is a trivial incident, it is an example of how rational assessment can moderate actions by overriding the first promptings of feelings
and so modify the course of action. We can leap to the other end of the
spectrum to find issues of national and international importance where
rationality has not been greatly in evidence and results have been parlous.
In 1995 Barings Bank collapsed and a *Times* leader introduced its comment
on the report of the Board of Banking Supervision in the following way:

'The report of the Board of Banking Supervision into the circumstances
surrounding the collapse of Britain's oldest merchant bank makes
breathtaking reading. The scale and breadth of the incompetence – at
Barings, in the Bank of England, and at the auditors – almost defies
imagination.'

Strong words. It was a spectacular collapse, and there have since been other financial transgressions of a similar scale without the companies concerned going under, because they have had greater resources. Interesting, though, how leaders of the business community get themselves into such dire straits. Our censure should not be reserved for business leaders, however, because the same issue of the *Times* had an article on the catalogue of mistakes made by the world's leading politicians on the Bosnian war. Retrospective analysis imparts a certain advantage, but it would be hard to contend convincingly that international co-operation on the Bosnian situation was a model of rationality. Then there was the British government's mishandling of the BSE crisis, which can be put down to almost total incompetence in managing, so called, scientific evidence. These are examples of the pinnacles of human folly but, at a lower level, events of a similar kind occur daily in organisations throughout the world. It would be naive to assume that all such errors could be eliminated, but it would seem reasonable to target the grossest stupidities. The question arises as to whether rationality has a role to play. Any role it does have must lie within the individual mind, but we can hardly expect its benefits to emerge in optimum form without some cultural encouragement. There is a natural capacity within the human brain for language, but individuals only become competent in linguistic expression if they are exposed to the right environment. We can see in our schools and other teaching institutions that great weight is placed on linguistic achievement, but where can we identify our formal training in rationality? We have to concede that there is little agreement about what is involved in the task or how to proceed if we wanted to.

Back to the Brain

It is easier to be rational when nothing is at stake personally because the higher cerebral processes of the brain are not so readily disrupted by emotional signals. One way of looking at rationality is to think of it as comprising neural maps which are interacting and competing with neural maps emerging from the limbic system, aided and abetted by its connections to the autonomic nervous system and prefrontal cortex. We have already seen that Antonio Damasio has provided evidence that patients with frontal lobe damage have emotional deficiencies and that those deficiencies mar their ability to plan and reason. It is as though the prefrontal cortices monitor and evaluate rational thought processes and then link these into the emotional circuits of the subcortex in order that a decision can be made; often at the unconscious level it would seem. To develop a highly simplified and schematic model for thinking about where rationality might fit into cerebral processes, it is useful once again to go back to our three blocks of the brain, though we have to recognise that they are all interdependent and interlinked with one another in a complex fashion. You will remember the subcortex comprises the thalamus, limbic system, basal ganglia and reticular formation, which can be likened to a *power source* which feeds the rest of the brain. Francis Crick has called the thalamus and its associated nuclei an *attentional searchlight*. The rate and nature of neuronal firing generated by the structures of the subcortex undoubtedly have an important influence on mental activity, but what determines the firing pattern is still unclear. It may be something to do with the intrinsic cell metabolism of neurons, or the level and distribution of neurotransmitters, or something else. This is an area where we have to wait for neuroscience to make progress. If the subcortex is the true energy source of the brain, then we can ally a highly active subcortex to restless, questing minds which seek satiety in a constant diet of stimulus and involvement. You should have no difficulty in recognising persons with this sort of mental disposition, and the fact that there is often a high emotional component associated with their activity. It doesn't say anything about their judgement or their ability to perceive events in an objective manner. At the other end of our distribution curve there will be placid minds where the energising influence of the subcortex is much lower, producing the mental tortoise compared with the mental hare. But it may be that when higher mental processes are employed they are not disrupted to the same extent by internal emotional signals. Some of these attributes can be identified with Frankie and Johnnie.

Our various perceptions of the external world are processed in the sensory cortex – the parieto–occipito–temporal lobes which, as well as handling sound and vision, also process language and our sense of structure and space. We know that perceptions and our linguistic ability can be severely impaired if there is damage to this part of the brain. The sensory cortex is heavily influenced by the subcortex because of its involvement in generating our feelings and determining the things we attend to and gain satisfaction from. The level of computation required in the sensory cortex to form our picture of the world, through sound, vision and touch, is immense and the only general agreement on how the brain binds it all together is that massive, parallel neural maps are involved. How this neuronal activity becomes translated into what we know as conscious awareness is one of the great unsolved riddles. The fact that the computation circuits are so complex, and that they are influenced by processing in the subcortex, means that there is likely to be considerable variation in what each of us perceives.

That variation will increase as the complexity of what we observe increases – the difference between looking at a chair and watching a Wagner opera. For all practical purposes we can assume that each of us sees a chair in the same way, but in any activity which involves emotional values and a temporal intermingling of events, the spread of perceptions is likely to be wide. Here lies one of the great differences between the computers we experience in every-day life and the mind. These computers are entirely digital devices in that, not only are their internal processors digital, but also their inputs and outputs are digital, preserving great accuracy and consistency. The brain has to deal with analogue signals, analogue processing, and analogue outputs. When digital electronic devices have to contend with analogue/digital conversions, they become subject to the same sorts of variations. Although I think all CD players sound the same, I doubt I would be able to convince the young hi-fi community of that fact!

The frontal cortex does not receive information from the physical world but it has direct links with the subcortex and sensory cortex and it may be thought of as an evaluator, which provides insights into our own behaviour and enables us to plan for the future and to achieve lasting intentions. What knowledge we have of frontal lobe activity comes from neuropsychology. There is only a limited amount that neuroscience can tell us about frontal cortex, now or in the foreseeable future, because it involves a level of activity largely confined to humans, on whom invasive experiments cannot be performed. We do know from neuropsychology that the frontal cortex is involved with working memory and has a role in assessing and evaluating our thought processes. We can assume that it is an important centre for rationality, though in the end it has to operate through the emotional centres in the subcortex, for this is where our feelings reside and decisions are eventually made. In making such an assertion I am perhaps oversimplifying and moving beyond the bounds of a scientifically verifiable account, but it will serve as a model for guiding us through the jungle of mental variables associated with rationality. Models can always be changed as knowledge advances. My objective is to provide a framework with which to gain some insight into how other minds may differ from your own, and a bit of licence is required.

Rationality in Society

An initial task is to provide some calibration on how much influence emotional and rational factors have on our decisions. In Chapter 2 I developed the idea of a bell-shaped, population distribution curve which employed some rather arbitrary measures of rationality on realist/romantic and anecdotalist/structuralist axes, with the majority of the population having a fairly even balance of both sets of characteristics. After all, 68% fall within one standard deviation of the mean. Can we usefully relate such folk psychology differentiations to mental activity? In many spheres of personal life where relationships are dominant, probably not, because so many of our actions are governed by emotions and feelings. You may try to rationalise whether it is sensible for you and your partner to separate or get married, but in the end it is the way you feel about it which is going to determine the result. A totally rational brain might make the decision on the probability of a favourable outcome compared with all the other possible outcomes that are open – a difficult calculation to make considering all the unknowns. We can therefore largely discount the role of conscious rationality in personal relationships: it's feelings that count. However, we should not forget the evidence from neuropsychology that the frontal lobes have an important role in determining feelings, which they could well modulate as a result of unconscious rational calculations.

The further we look beyond the purely personal sphere, the more it is possible to make a case for the benefits of greater overt rationality, in the sense that it means making a judgement on a realistic appraisal of the evidence and making an assessment of the risks of being wrong. It means subjecting impulses to proper scrutiny and, to a degree, it becomes a conscious, intellectual activity. We can imagine a dominant neural map centred in the sensory cortex, occasioned by some kind of external event, being processed as much through coupled neural maps in frontal cortex as through coupled neural maps in the subcortex. It is not an uncommon experience in every-day life to be aware of the conflict that can arise between our rational assessment of a situation and the emotions it generates. Let's take a topical example – road rage. Many of us become exasperated, when we are driving our cars, by the perceived incompetence of other drivers or by the Department of Transport's lack of consideration in allowing road works which result in five-mile tail-backs. I get particularly upset by traffic jams on motorways, because of the sense of being trapped, and I have a quiet, or not so quiet, rant to myself. I know I am being irrational, but it helps to relieve my feelings. I am never so irrational that I try and take it out on someone else, although my passenger might challenge this conclusion. We know this is a crowded, little country and traffic is going to get worse rather than better. It would be a pity for society if the majority of us surrendered to aggressive feelings and let them affect our behaviour. Inevitably, there will be some who lose control, but we must surely hope they will be few and far between. There is another insight we can get from observing car drivers, particularly when parking their cars. In choosing a parking place, considerate persons will automatically make some rational assessment of how they may affect others, even if in the end they decide to put their own interests first and take the risk of parking obstructively. Would you believe that some people park without such a thought entering their heads?

Thought which makes any claim to conscious rationality obviously has to rise above the emotional level and the purely self-centred, though self-interest is a perfectly valid consideration to fit into the equation. We must allow the organism to seek long-term survival in the most propitious circumstances achievable. The test is whether the predicted outcome is the one attained. If behaving irrationally always ended up with the right result, there would be no case for rationality. We are all a mixture of the rational and the irrational, even the great leaders of history, where the evidence suggests their lives tend to end in failure because irrationality overcomes them. The distorting influences of success and power are immense. Who could have been more rational than Napoleon in his early years, charismatic though he was? Then he invades Russia and sacrifices thousands of lives because his ego has blown rational calculation out of the window. The experience is repeated time and time again, even in modern times, so the evidence suggests we have learned little. Great leaders are people of conviction, and they become successful leaders because their convictions happen to match the times. If they are out of step with the times then they have little chance, whatever their qualities. As soon as the times move on they quickly pass their sell-by date, and by this time any rationality they possessed has probably been terminally damaged. It may be difficult to prove this assertion by retrospective analysis, because events can be made to fit many ways, and it would be even more difficult to organise a prospective study.

However, let's get back to the hum-drum, every-day world. The brain is an extraordinarily complex organ with a vast range of options open to it in terms of processing neuronal signals. No matter how long mankind inhabits the earth, there will never be two brains that process thoughts in an identical manner. The passage of time alone will see to that. Is there any point, then, in trying to draw out threads which give insight into the way minds operate? A good test of that is whether such an approach produces results of practical value. I am going to stick my neck out and look at the mind as though there is a degree of conscious conflict between emotionality and rationality, which could be caricatured as subcortex dominance versus frontal cortex, though we know it really isn't as simple as that. We have already seen in earlier discussions that emotions (in which I include feelings) give us a short cut to decisions. We *feel* something is right, and we act on it: we don't need to agonise over a long analysis of all the options and work out the probabilities; we sense them. It may well be that there are unconscious processes of rational analysis which help us reach our feeling for a decision and which involve neural maps vastly in excess of the number that ever reach the level of consciousness. If there is such a deployment of neural resources it will be because it has had evolutionary value. But so often our feelings let us down when we tackle complex issues outside our immediate experience. This sort of situation occurs frequently in large organisations, and so to illustrate the point and exemplify what can happen in the world around us we will have a look at the company Frankie and Johnnie work for – Mindspace Co.

Mindspace Co., a global company specialising in workspace problems, is interested in taking over a high-tech competitor called Neuromap Ltd, whose share price has been rising rapidly. There are market rumours that Neuromap is on to a breakthrough in re-entrant maps. Frankie is in Finance and Johnnie in Product Strategy so they are both in a working party the Chief Executive of Mindspace has set up to study the acquisition proposal. The team leader is the Marketing Director, who is known to be particularly ambitious and, like most people who have come up through Sales, he is an enthusiast and an optimist. Frankie likes him, but Johnnie thinks his judgement is suspect. The Research Director has been asked to provide a technical evaluation of Neuromap's product portfolio and to evaluate future prospects for its research pipeline. Based on this technical evaluation, Frankie and Johnnie have to produce sales and profit projections with discounted cash-flow returns. They both recognise that producing forecasts of this sort requires a lot of imagination, laced with considerable uncertainty. Consequently, their projections are suitably qualified with probabilities on the break-even point for various acquisition prices, and it is clear they have difficulty in justifying a bid premium on Neuromap's current market value. Although they would like a cautious conclusion to the working party paper, the Marketing Director decides on a positive recommendation to acquire.

The Board of Directors considers the acquisition paper along with its other business and has to base its decision on the figures in the paper. The Chief Executive, a man of strong will, is looking for confirmation of his own belief that the acquisition is viable, and the Marketing Director is keen to make the right impression on his board colleagues as a dynamic individual. He chooses to ignore the cautionary comments of the working party. It has to be said that Johnnie is more pessimistic about merger prospects than Frankie. The acquisition proposal is approved and the purchase price of Neuromap eventually proves to be higher than Mindspace Co.'s highest estimate. Results from Neuromap's re-entrant map work are much further away than expected and the merged company soon finds its financial performance compromised. The Chief Executive is not at all pleased and blames the working party for its poor projections. Of course, it is his own irrationality which is at fault. Because of his enthusiasm he failed to place adequate emphasis on the uncertainties and took the Marketing Director's confident assurances at face value. The Marketing Director has since taken early retirement.

All organisations are a mixture of enthusiasm and caution, of the rational and irrational. It is just as easy for over-caution to be irrational as over-enthusiasm, so it is often quite difficult to determine where the truth lies. Many times it is impossible to be confident about matters until the emergent-algorithm has run its course, and so correct diagnosis is at a premium. Clues can be obtained from individual personalities. Dominance traits are often associated with overactive centres of assertion and aggression, and this should immediately put us on our guard that emotion and rationality may not be in balance. It can also prove difficult to weigh-up the effects of different cultures. During my own business experience I came into contact with colleagues in other businesses within my own company, where the culture was quite different to the one in which I worked; so much so that I often felt I needed an interpreter to decipher what was intended by their words. There seemed to be a courtly tip-toeing around the thoughts they really wanted to express, compared with the straightforward inter-change I was accustomed to. This quite often led to misunderstandings. Perhaps, as much as anything else, this led me to a realisation of how much words can cover up thoughts, and how imprecise they are as a means of communication, despite the marvellous mechanism which lies behind them. In applying a principle of rationality, it becomes essential to get at the thought behind the words, but in daily life we are rarely in a position to do this. After all, we cannot cross-question everybody we speak to. In a business, though, chief executives are in a much stronger position because of their hierarchical position, though they rarely take advantage of it. How many mistakes could be avoided if they were only able to step down from the stratosphere of their egos and find out what people really thought? Given the chance, it may be that more women in the senior ranks of industry could add a beneficial angle to the rational aspects of corporate performance because they seem to be less troubled by egocentric and aggressive behaviour.

If communication in business presents its difficulties in applying ration-ality, then that in politics must present an almost insurmountable obstacle. At least most people in a publicly quoted company are pulling in the same direction. The political scene is such a maelstrom of vested interests that the number of agendas being played out is virtually boundless, and it is not surprising that businessmen often flounder when they enter the political arena. Politicians take a perverse pride in this situation, because it obviously says something about the resilience of the survivors, and it can be assumed, without much fear of contradiction, that they do not rate rationality very highly. There is no evidence, that I am aware, that intrinsic levels of rationality are lower in politicians than the population at large, it is just that the adversarial nature of the game puts a premium on other characteristics. If rationality is very low on the survival agenda in politics, it would seem to undermine its chances as an evolutionary cultural force, and a survey of the world scene gives much ground for such pessimism. If this is ever to change we have to make a start in being able to identify what to look for.

It is ironic that many of the verbal correlates of rationality do not constitute permissible forms of expression in public life. For instance, the willingness to admit mistakes when things go wrong, as they are bound to do, or a declaration of something less than certainty about a central issue, let alone an acknowledgement occasionally of some merit in an opposing point of view. Any leader adopting these stances would soon be devoured by the rat-pack of the media, and the opposition would play the situation for all it was worth. Perhaps, politicians are not so irrational after all! For standards to change, the electorate has to become much more enlightened in recognising and valuing rationality, and that is a matter of education. The size of the problem immediately becomes apparent. But there is also another consideration: that the rich tapestry of life is enhanced by the antics of individualists, of characters and eccentrics, where there is no apparent connection with rational behaviour.

This brings us down to the bedrock of the rationality issue – deciding the basis on which we need to move forward. The examples I have cited merely illustrate the dilemmas confronting us, and I would now like to suggest a possible approach towards resolution. If we all decided to behave rationally all the time it would make the world a much duller place, and I would hate to be the promoter of that idea. Let's assume we are allowed to continue behaving and believing in our traditional manner, but we accept the challenge of trying to differentiate, without prejudice, between the rational and the irrational, and deciding where they fit in the equation of our lives. There is no constraint on anyone's belief or behaviour, no value judgement to be made, just a need to tune up our faculties to recognise whether we, or others, are acting in a more or less romantic or realist fashion. The design space for belief and behaviour, to borrow a concept from Daniel Dennett[2], is so immense that we have to narrow down our frame of reference to something we can discuss sensibly and without the distorting factor of unnecessary emotion. Politics and religion obviously do not fit the bill. I suggest that *health* provides a suitable substrate for examination.

Applying Rationality to Health

We are all interested in our own health, and we would like to remain in the best of health for as long as possible. I do not expect much dissension from this point of view. And yet many of us behave in a way which we know is likely to damage our health in the long run. We eat too much, drink too much alcohol, smoke, fail to take sufficient exercise and, in extreme instances, resort to drugs. While, in some instances this may be attributed to ignorance, there are many who indulge with their eyes wide open. Let me say straight away that I am not setting myself on a pulpit, since my love of wine ensures I consume more than the recommended maximum number of units of alcohol a week. However, I do watch such indicators as my weight and my blood pressure. There is now sufficient evidence for us to accept the statistical correlations between unhealthy practices and the incidence of morbidity and mortality as a result of them. There are many doctors who smoke and who are aware of the risks they incur, yet they continue the practice. Of course they realise there is a statistically increased chance of lung cancer, but they are also able to calculate the odds and decide to take the risk. That, at least, is the rational point of view. It may also be that they feel that life isn't worth living without being able to smoke, the stimulant effect of nicotine being indispensable.

For those who drink alcohol in some form the same calculation applies. Cardiovascular, cerebral and liver disease can all result from excessive consumption. The government has specified a safe limit, and many ignore it, including myself. Part of the reason is the recognition that any scientific basis for the limit has been heavily modified by political considerations. Nevertheless, there is a clear limit to what is sensible for each individual, depending on bodyweight and metabolic profile, which symptomatic evidence will indicate and which many choose to ignore. This may be associated with sleep patterns, sexual activity, memory performance, weight gain, facial skin tone, cardiovascular symptoms, liver enlargement or a combination of several of these. And yet someone who is aware of these factors might decide on a trade-off. Alcoholism is reported as being quite prevalent within the medical profession. Where does the rational stance lie? Certainly it would be irrational to deny that there is an association between excessive alcohol intake and certain symptoms, though cause and effect is always difficult to prove in an individual, and it can be denied more readily than a statistical conclusion about the population. Couldn't we say that the rational stance for all of us is to follow the government guidelines? Yes, we could, but we know that will carry no weight with a large sector of the population, because the pleasure of alcohol outweighs the theoretical risks based on a superficial assessment of the evidence.

What is the rational stance towards smoking and alcohol? Some will be in favour of banning both, claiming that we would all be healthier without them, despite the fact there is evidence in favour of moderate alcohol consumption. However, historical experience suggests that prohibition introduces even larger problems, as it has done with addictive drugs. We have to recognise an innate desire for palliative neuropharmacological experiences within a large sector of the population. Should we ban tea and coffee because of their stimulant effects, and even chocolate? Perhaps sexual activity outside the act of procreation is also undesirable because it over-exercises the nervous system and can lead to alarming rises in blood pressure. It would be a dull life if we proscribed everything that could possibly do us harm, and it is reassuring that a democratic society makes the chances of that happening very remote indeed. But we still need to decide where to draw the line on self-injurious behaviour. The trouble is that population variation makes that line a difficult one to draw – your poison may be my harmless euphoriant.

The ideal situation would be to leave it to the individual. But suppose I find life unbearable without stimulant A or sedative B; how do I reconcile considerations of my long-term health with my day-to-day feelings and their need for a little external help? I suggest rationality provides an approach towards countering the most self-injurious tendencies of desire for immediate gratification and the belief that no harm will ensue. Our folk psychology terms of *belief* and *desire* arise again in connection with the generation of *feelings*. Whatever the neural processes going on in our brains it does seem possible to construct a useful model which views these mental properties as being in dynamic equilibrium with *rationality*. Our beliefs about our health have to be based on medical evidence. Most people are not in a position to evaluate that evidence with the same rigour as a government authority, so official pronouncements do have an important status. People decide to believe or not to believe, and they may seek other sources of information to bolster their stance. But that belief is also influenced by the level of desire to behave in a certain way. If the desire is strong there will be an incentive to interpret the evidence in a way most congruent with that desire and, as we all know, there are always at least two sides to a statistical argument. Where does the desire spring from? Not many would deny feelings an important role. Feelings can influence desire, and desire can influence belief. Where does rationality come in? Well, at least it can help you realise what is going on. This analysis may sound rather simplistic, but can it be denied that in order to get a higher fidelity picture of the true state of mental interactions, rationality has to be deployed? If rationality isn't deployed we may find ourselves in a state of self-delusion, where feelings and desires distort our beliefs.

The nature of belief, then, has rational and emotional components and it should not be difficult to identify people among your acquaintances who are over-concerned about aspects of their health, as well as those who fail to recognise that the habits they indulge in are probably injurious. Many are not in a position to make a rational assessment of the evidence and have to rely on their inner feelings unless they undergo a thorough medical investigation. Even procedures of this sort have only a certain probability of pin-pointing the right diagnosis because of the complicated interactions of bodily systems and the fallibility of examiners. It seems uncertainty surrounds us even in the case of our own health, so how much more uncertain is the influence of social interactions on our lives? This uncertainty is probably the overriding reason for reliance on feelings and belief: rational analysis is just far too complicated and quite often it ends up with the wrong answer because the facts are incomplete. The emergent-algorithm of life is truly chaotic and the legacy of our forebears can have totally unforeseen consequences in the long term.

Evolution of Rationality

Our ability to foresee the consequences of our actions is severely limited, largely because we are not able to build into our calculations the effect of all the known variables with sufficient accuracy, let alone all the unknowns. This sounds as though it could be a formula for stalemate and inaction, though I do not think it need be. If we look at the theatre of politics we see that policies are generally driven by strong beliefs; beliefs in which the component of rationality may be quite small, with the result that various disasters abound. If we were living in a rational world we could only give a particular policy a certain probability of achieving the expected outcome. In such a society it may be that the government of the day would pursue policies that it gave a greater than 50% chance of achieving a stated target, or it may set itself a higher 70% hurdle, and then be judged on its track record. There would be nothing to stop us pursuing policies on the basis of a judgement of the probabilities with equal vigour to that related to the irrational convictions of dogmatic belief. Obviously, there would be practical limitations in implementing such a strategy because of the difficulties and ambiguities in judging results, but just think of the impact it could have on the realism of political outlook if people were educated to think in this way. It isn't as though this would be advocating some totally artificial way of looking at political outcomes; it does in fact correspond more closely to the realities of life. Despite all the evidence confronting us we are largely blind to the uncertainties surrounding our long-term fate, and we will not fully appreciate the realities until an understanding and a respect for rationality is built into our educational processes.

It has taken the human brain six million years to evolve to its present state[3], though it arrived at more or less its present form some 100,000 years ago. Recorded history for our species only stretches back 5000 years, and in evolutionary terms we have the same brains to cope with modern technological complexity as we had in setting up primitive agricultural communities 10,000 years ago. Do our brains have the capability of withstanding the bombardment of sensory information which will be an increasing characteristic of the future, and what capacities will it require? In a span of only 200 years we have passed from an age when there was no motive power, so no one had travelled faster than a horse on land, and people were confined to long dark evenings with candles or oil lamps and a deathless absence of sound or vision – to an age when we whiz around at great speed and electronic gadgetry bombards everyone with a multitude of stimuli, all day and every day. Two hundred years is a blink in terms of biological evolutionary time, but obviously quite significant on a cultural scale. The individual mind cannot do much about the chaotic impact of events, but it surely has to be trained if it is to remain stable and grow into new areas of competence.

Some geneticists and evolutionary biologists believe that the evolution of the human brain has finished in a biological sense, but others disagree. Even if the biological evolution of mankind has finished it seems likely that cultural evolution will continue. The geneticist, R. C. Lewontin[4], has postulated that human genes may have ceded their right to determine evolution and surrendered their power to social interaction. If we accept that this is the case, what do we suppose the dominant influences will be? There are many candidates, but we cannot ignore what some eminent scientists have characterised as the highest form of human evolution – self-awareness and its link to social behaviour. Only the algorithm of cultural evolution can give us the result which will emerge from competitive social pressures, but a starting point is to examine the correlation of culture with technological progress, because the evidence suggests that technology is closely related to economic performance. History does seem to indicate that good economic performance is a necessary attribute to get through the qualifying rounds in the competition for high pecking order among nations. Will those societies that encourage rationality do better than those who ignore it? Will those that subjugate the interests of the individual to the interests of the group do better than those who give free reign to individualism and even fanaticism? Perhaps there is a need to develop a rationality quotient for societies so that progress can be correlated against this measure.

The freedom to develop as an individual is a highly prized characteristic of many societies and it would be nice to see it as part of the formula for economic success. However, we cannot ignore the evidence that suggests there is increasingly an inverse correlation as technological prowess becomes dependent on the group. Those societies which emphasise conformity and teamwork appear to reap the greater reward. This isn't at all surprising. Suppose the neurons in our brains were allowed to 'do their own thing' regardless of what other neurons were doing: it is likely that our brains would remain totally confused. Perhaps we have to find new measures for human achievement which are related to team effort, but which allow us to live on more than one plane. Roger Scruton[5] is a philosopher who has stressed the importance of *individual essence* and has deplored the fact that science does not appear to recognise it. But he misunderstands science, which is only a technique that allows us to get our bearings on matters of natural fact and helps to determine the probability of outcomes. Where outcomes are unimportant, or we are not concerned with natural processes, we are free to revel in our own individual essence. We have to learn to live life in one compartment as a team-player and in another as an individual.

One of the joys of retirement is that you can respond to no one's agenda but your own. Even if you are the boss of a large organisation or a leading politician your life is determined by other people's agendas. It's the perceived interests of shareholders, voters, customers, competitors, political opponents, media Mafiosi or your secretary which dictate activities. Even academics are corralled by their peers into political correctness and by funding agencies into particular areas of study. One of the few truly free persons is the pensioner, as long as he or she has a decent pension. But pensioners do not determine economic performance, though they can still try to make a contribution. It is the idea of contribution to society and its relationship to *self-awareness* that I would like to examine in the next chapter. This centres on the concept that everybody should feel themselves capable of making a contribution to the evolution of society, no matter how small, because in the end it is the one identifiable judgement that can be made on our transient existence as a member of the species *Homo sapiens sapiens*. Who could put it better than George Eliot when she is writing about Dorothea at the end of *Middlemarch*:

> 'Her finely-touched spirit had still its fine issues, though they were not widely visible. Her full nature, like that river of which Cyrus broke the strength, spent itself in channels which had no great name on the earth. But the effect of her being on those around her was incalculably diffusive: for the growing good of the world is partly dependent on unhistoric acts; and that things are not so ill with you and me as they might have been, is half owing to the number who lived faithfully a hidden life, and rest in unvisited tombs.'

Chapter 7

Self-awareness and Other Minds

Frankie and Johnnie have shared a flat for about five years and have got to know each others' foibles pretty well. One thing that has always remained a puzzle to Johnnie, though, is Frankie's mood first thing in the morning. Normally talkative and effervescent, she can appear quite sullen early in the morning. At first Johnnie thought it was something he had said or done which had upset her, but he soon came to realise that it was a mental phase quite independent of his behaviour. He once attempted to probe her mood to see if there were feelings which brought on the change in character, but he received the response, 'I don't know what you're talking about; I feel fine'. And there the conversation ended. Johnnie concluded that it would be wiser not to pursue the matter and observation over a long period has convinced him that Frankie is not aware of feeling any different during her morning bouts of diminished communicativeness. It seems she is simply more reflective than usual and prefers her own thoughts to sharing them with others. With his more introspective temperament, Johnnie still finds it difficult to obtain any insight into Frankie's morning moods, especially as she doesn't recognise any special change in herself. It is obviously a tiny rock on which their relationship could founder, but it is one that is easy to accommodate with a little insight. Johnnie has really no idea what accounts for Frankie's fluctuation in character, especially as she doesn't admit to any conscious awareness of a change. He puts it down to her outgoing nature and an absence of fondness for introspection. He sometimes feels that his own self-consciousness is a cross he has to bear in establishing relationships with other people, while Frankie's unconcern allows her to establish friendships more readily.

Consciousness

Although it can be confidently stated that many animals experience consciousness, it is only in human beings that self-consciousness can be unequivocally established. Chimpanzees can demonstrate a degree of self-recognition, but there is no evidence that other animals can achieve even this rudimentary form of self-awareness. Non-humans do not question their own actions or wonder what it is about themselves that determines acceptance or non-acceptance by their companions. A newly born baby is obviously conscious, but self-awareness takes time to develop. In discussions of consciousness it is often apparent that consciousness and self-consciousness get confused. I will stick to the term 'self-awareness' so that it does not get muddled with any other aspects of consciousness, or with the psychological state of being overly-conscious of self. Consciousness itself is still a great mystery, and philosophers like Colin McGinn and Thomas Nagel believe that it will remain so for as long as human cognitive abilities remain at their present level. They do not adhere to a dualistic interpretation of mind involving belief in a spiritual world, but they accept limitations on man's explanatory capacities. Other philosophers, like Paul and Patricia Churchland, are convinced that neuroscience will one day offer an explanation for consciousness related to physical properties of the brain. All agree that we are not in sight of an explanation at the present time. There are those who try to dismiss consciousness as a non-issue, but they have not managed to recruit many adherents. In the current state of knowledge we will have to content ourselves with looking at some of the characteristics of consciousness and how they apply to self-awareness.

We all know that the difference between being awake and being asleep is something to do with consciousness. Although dreaming is regarded as a form of consciousness, because we can report on our experience, it is rather different to the consciousness we experience when fully awake. In a state of wakefulness we can direct our attention towards a chosen matter rather than be a passive follower of some outrageous sequence of events generated by neural activity in the sleeping brain. There is evidence that nuclei in the thalamus and their connections to the neocortex are intimately involved with consciousness. Rhythmic firing of these thalamic centres can be detected both during dreaming and during a state of wakefulness, but this says very little about the qualitative and quantitative nature of the neural mechanisms being activated. Investigative work is at a very early stage and so it may be many years before some of the immense complexities of neuronal firing patterns can be related to a particular state of consciousness. What we can say with a fair degree of confidence is that there is an intimate link between attentional mechanisms in the brain and conscious awareness, and we find the thalamus once again centre stage in directing attention. Like most parts of the brain, it never acts alone, so other subcortical and neocortical structures are involved, but neuroscience has not yet worked out the definitve relationships.

For our purposes we can simply view the arousal system of the brain as being based in the subcortex, and in this we share a common mechanism with other animals. We don't really know how the arousal system works, except that aminergic and cholinergic neurotransmitters in the reticular formations of the midbrain and thalamus are involved. The degree to which we are aroused, and when, has something to do with the body's basic metabolism. Neurons are surrounded by glial cells, which outnumber them 10:1, and they are perfused by a soup of organic molecules where an immense number of chemical reactions is taking place all the time. It is safe to assume that the miraculous biochemistry on which our lives depend is a classical example of a self-organising, complex adaptive system – to some extent under genetic control but also subject to the influence of environmental agents ingested in food and drink and the air we breath. It is hard to imagine a more non-linear system in the sense that it is difficult to predict what interference with any one tiny part of the mechanism will do, and yet the whole process sustains life for many years unless interfered with in a grossly damaging way. We can envisage consciousness as being dependent on neurons, but neurons soon cease to function if not provided with oxygen, water, essential ions such as K^+, Na^+ and Ca^{2+}, and many vital organic molecules.

Self-awareness is a category of consciousness which enables us to gain insight into our own thoughts, feelings, beliefs and desires, and to analyse how they interact with the world. We would be hard pressed to do this while dreaming since we need to employ the most highly developed centres of the brain in an analytical manner. The frontal cortex is almost certainly involved, though it needs to be activated by the arousal system and connected up with many other parts of the brain, including the limbic system in the subcortex. As we become adults, all of us develop a clear idea of what it is like to be ourselves, with our own egocentric perspectives on the world, our own self-interests, our medley of moods and relationships, and our hopes for the future. There is no evidence that other mammals, even the primates, have this pattern of mental activity. True self-awareness is almost certainly something uniquely human, and it may well be associated with the application of linguistic and rational analysis, providing the ability to form concepts which allow us to identify our role in the world and our place within the flow of time. Evidence from neuropsychology suggests that patients with frontal lobe damage lose their ability to place themselves strategically within their environment and to judge their own best interests. Although these patients can often perform satisfactorily in tests of memory or intelligence, they are unable to plan and structure their lives in a normal manner. It is as though an executive function, which integrates and interprets other mental activities, is missing. There is good reason to suppose that neocortex of the frontal lobes is crucial in obtaining an effective balance between rational and emotional evaluation of sensory inputs, and bringing that balance into conscious awareness.

We can, of course, be conscious at a much lower level. A sensation of a sound, the perception of a visual image, a sense of body warmth, are all things we can immediately identify with as conscious experiences. It is also easy for us to accept that feelings which accompany these experiences can be extended to other animals, and that they therefore have a form of consciousness. Only when we start to analyse our feelings and the thoughts they generate do we begin to sense a gulf developing between our species and all others. This power of analysis obviously depends on our more highly evolved neocortex, but underlying it there are still powerful feelings which have a much older evolutionary basis and which often have a determining influence on the direction our thoughts take. Whatever consciousness is, it seems to emerge below the level of thought and any dependence that thought may have on language. We know the amount of computation in the neocortex required to produce sensory experiences is immense, though it is still a mystery how the brain binds everything together to give us our effortless picture of our environment. It seems fair to assume that the neuronal networks required for thought are correspondingly massive and involve extensive areas of the brain. Thinking invariably involves beliefs and the memories which generate them. Because both beliefs and memories are unique to the individual, they are inaccessible to analysis on a population basis. This leads to different theories on how the mind works. There are theories which regard the mind as modular, so that thoughts are processed in distinct modules in the brain; others favour the idea of a global workspace. Some theorists regard language as the basis of thought, and some are convinced that it is not. If we could each analyse how we think and pool the results we might make some headway, but that would call for an exceptional level of self-awareness and a degree of analytical precision which is not available. Despite this handicap, my aim in this chapter is to offer a working model of the mind which might be helpful in understanding your own mind and gaining an insight into the makeup of others.

A Model of Mind

It is beyond dispute that there are modules in the mind. We can identify the primary visual cortex in the occipital lobe, the auditory cortex in the superior temporal lobe, the somatosensory cortex in the anterior parietal lobe, and the language areas in the left hemisphere. These are clearly specialised areas of the brain, though they will vary in significant detail from one person to another and changes may even be observed within an individual if there is injury to a part of the body mapped on to the cortex. The question remains, though, as to how these specialised areas play their part in the higher functions of the brain. A useful clue can be obtained from work that has been carried out on motor functions in the brain – those that control muscular movement. Sensing the position of our limbs, preparing for movement, and then carrying it out requires immense computation within the central nervous system. Billions of neurons are involved. The evidence suggests that no one neuron or group of neurons is in control, but each neuron involved has a vote in making its contribution to muscular control. Democracy prevails in the brain! The majority vote results in what researchers have called a *population vector* or *population coding*[1]. Although analogies to human populations earlier in this book may have seemed somewhat fanciful, there may well be more aptness to them than you first realised. The clearest evidence of population coding comes from the superior colliculus – a part of the mid-brain which controls saccadic movements of the eyes. A portion of the retinal output in optic nerve neurons projects to the superior colliculus, which contains both a sensory map and a motor map for the eyes. When a point of light registers on the retina and the eye has to move to bring it into focus, the resultant saccade is determined by the outcome of neuronal population coding within the superior colliculus. What a marvellous mechanism this is. Proper working of eye movement does not depend on one neuronal pathway being in tip-top working order, but on the collaboration of millions of neurons. If some fail or become redundant, others can take over.

It is likely to be many years before scientists can work out whether the population-coding principle apples to cognitive activities of the brain, but it does give us a working basis for thinking about the mind. The principle has already been used for developing a theory of memory[2]. Although certain parts of the brain, like the hippocampus and frontal cortex, can be associated with memory, no evidence has been elicited on *how* the brain stores memories. No encoding or *engram* has been identified. The theory I refer to envisages that parts of a memory are stored widely throughout the brain and it is only when populations of neurons come together in firing patterns that we can retrieve memories. It is unlikely that an individual neuron or neuronal assembly can store a complete memory. Furthermore, storage of memories is envisaged to be something of a random process; it depends on which neurons were paying attention at the time. The more neurons there are involved, the more likely it is a memory will be encoded. An overwhelming emotional experience is likely to engage a vast area in the brain resulting in firmly implanted episodic memory. This is the 'remembering where you were when Kennedy was shot' syndrome. Even if there is validity in this model it is not possible to say how neurons retain a record in order that they can contribute to the total memory. A favourite candidate for memory engrams is newly synthesised protein at synaptic receptor sites, but it could be other organic molecules within the cell, the glial cells surrounding the neurons, or just configurations of neurons. It is impossible to guess confidently at the present time.

The model I am going to employ extends the idea of neuronal population coding to other properties of the thinking mind. Conscious awareness itself may simply be a feature of the dominant firing pattern of a neuronal population in the brain, as has already been suggested with the idea of the 'dominant gestalt', but in assessing other minds it is perhaps more fruitful to consider the interplay between variables like *rationality*, *beliefs* and *feelings*. Here we can usefully go back to our human population analogy, because the same forces may well be at work. A society with a population of many millions has far fewer voters than the brain with its tens of billions of neurons, and it also works on a different timescale – weeks and years rather than milliseconds and seconds. And yet, the manner in which a society reaches its point of view has to do with the aggregate view of individuals, though some will be more influential than others. We don't know if some neurons in the brain have more influence than others, but in the end it is reasonable to assume that there will be a prevailing neuronal opinion – some firing patterns will have gained ascendancy over others. The model I wish to introduce assumes that feelings are determined by one set of neurons and that they can be modulated by a quite different set.

In evolutionary terms it is reasonable to consider that feelings occupy the most basic circuits in the brain and are the driving force for much action. Most of us do not have first-hand experience of our nearest evolutionary neighbour, the chimpanzee, but we can see that our pets are affected by feelings. We can envisage the family poodle climbing onto the back of a chair near the lounge window every afternoon at around 4 p.m. when the children are due home from school. What is it that makes it do this? Surely not a thought process of a human kind. The dog perceives the routine in the house as the mistress is starting to cook, it is aware of shadows falling in a certain direction, and perhaps a clock chimes. The combination of these events produces a feeling that it is a certain time of day and the children of the household should be home soon. Of course, we have no way of knowing what is going on in the mind of the poodle, but I hope it is possible to agree that its actions could be determined by feelings without any need for thought which analyses the various perceived events in a rational fashion. This is the *default model* which I introduced at the end of Chapter 3. In the absence of competition from other neuronal populations it is the neural correlate of feelings which determines actions. Where do these neural correlates lie? We know that the subcortex and the autonomic nervous system are involved, but what about the neocortex?

Antonio Damasio has demonstrated quite convincingly that the frontal cortex is involved in the determination of feelings, but what has not been elucidated is how resolution of feelings is achieved. Let's assume for the moment that the frontal cortex is the main centre of the brain concerned with rational deliberation and that there are alignments of neurons which are able to analyse events and come to a rational judgement. Whatever the process employed it will not be able to analyse sufficient facts to come to a completely logical conclusion, because there never are enough facts available. In the end the judgement has to be made on a balance of probabilities, and the only process that can crystallise that judgement within the human mind is a feeling. It may seem that we have a circular argument here, but I do not think this is the case. The interaction of rational analysis and feelings is absolutely crucial in determining the population result of neuronal activity. Let's once again look at a human society trying to make a decision on an important national issue, and we could take European monetary union. Should the U.K. be in or out? There is obviously no absolute answer because we do not know what the future will bring. We made a decision not to join the European Economic Community in the 1950s, and that turned out to be a bad choice. This is not the place to go into the pros and cons of monetary union, but it is quite likely that you have feelings on the matter. How did these feelings arise, and on what facts are they based? Have you recently read an adverse article in a Eurosceptic tabloid which has set your indignation aboil? Clearly, it is possible to analyse the matter and the manner in which your opinions have been formed. The way this is done will depend on whether you are a member of the government or a bystander, and what personal agenda you have. We might think of the process of examining our own convictions as *meta-analysis*, because we are looking at the process by which we come to our judgement, as well as making the judgement itself. It certainly requires self-awareness.

The decision on whether the UK should be part of European monetary union will eventually be taken by the government of the day, which is likely to seek a mandate by means of a referendum – in effect a population vote on the issue. The views of individuals will be determined by a whole host of considerations, both rational and irrational, and feelings are sure to run high. There will be arguments about economic interest and national sovereignty, which many people will be unable to resolve in their own minds because the issues are so complicated and the outcomes so uncertain. In the end everyone who votes will end up with a belief on the issue and will vote on the basis of that belief. We could plot a distribution curve of those beliefs if we could get at the information. Some will be strongly for and others strongly against, but the majority is likely to fall somewhere in the middle, so that most people will vote with a degree of uncertainty in their minds and without strong convictions.

In truth it is very difficult to decide the right course of action on the basis of economic judgement because no one knows how monetary union will affect Europe in 10 years' time. It looks likely that more fundamental issues surrounding national emotion will determine the result. This can be seen as analogous to the process in the individual brain because, whenever a person thinks about the issue, populations of neurons will be making their contribution to the neuronal maps which will have a decisive say in the big decision. There will be rational maps and emotional maps; memory maps and sensory maps, all interacting with one another. The way self-awareness can help is that it can assist in meta-analysis – enabling you to know why you voted the way you did.

The one thing rationality cannot provide in this instance is the 'right' answer, because that will not be known for many years until the emergent-algorithm has run its course. It is quite possible that a tide of emotion will produce a result that we will later come to regret, but who can say with any degree of confidence? The one thing that rationality will do is allow you to make a judgement on the uncertainties. Is there a greater than 50% chance that monetary union could be in the economic interests of the UK? Almost certainly, yes. Is there a greater than 50% chance that parliamentary sovereignty will be seriously eroded? Probably, yes, and some may put it as high as 90%. Does it matter? Is the bureaucracy in Brussels off the rails? Probably, yes. Does it matter? Are Germany and France conspiring to dominate Europe and will they eventually fall out with dire consequences? How do you weigh these issues one against another? And so on. In the end each person has to decide what is most important to them, and they can only do this by consciously considering all the issues. Some people will be more informed than others, some better able to carry out analysis than others. Our objective in this chapter is not to make a decision on Europe but to understand what is going on in our own and other people's minds. We can only do this if we have some means of gauging the balance of forces at work, and that means having a working model of the mind.

Frankie is unable to understand Johnnie's Euroscepticism. With her financial background and involvement in the European subsidiaries of Mindspace Co. she sees that it is obviously in the interests of the UK to participate fully in Europe. Besides, she likes her French, German and Italian colleagues, with whom she has most dealings, and she trusts their integrity. British politicians, she believes, have little understanding of Europe because their world is in the House of Commons, which they have difficulty in seeing beyond. In any case, their agendas are set more by their own ambitions than by consideration of any long-term interests of Britain. She cannot understand why Johnny doesn't see it this way. The two of them have their debates and agree on many things, but Johnny really doesn't come clean. He knows that he is emotionally against further federation moves in Europe because he is appalled by what he sees of the vast Brussels' bureaucracy. It has taken on a life of its own and is not held accountable in a rigorous manner. The European Parliament is little more than a rubber stamp, and in any case it is manipulated by naked, national self-interest. He sees the manipulation going on all the time, and he see British interests constantly out-manoeuvred. He thinks the British are not devious enough to operate effectively in Europe and they do not have the same petulant self-interest as some other member countries. It's all right Frankie going on about her colleagues in Mindspace Co., but they are part of the same team and subject to the hierarchy of the organisation. Of course they are easy and pleasant to deal with. She should try dealing with competitors in his product area, where there is no governing hierarchy in a strong, international company. He knows how Frankie feels about her colleagues and has therefore been cautious in expressing his views. He knows the way he is going to vote though, and why.

The *model of mind* I am proposing assumes that we reach conscious decisions through competition between neuronal populations in the brain, with a winner-takes-all result. This is very much in line with the 'dominant gestalt' theory proposed by a number of neuroscientists when they speculate about consciousness. I am taking the process one step further in envisaging that there is a balanced interaction in mental processes between rationality and emotion. There is no question that emotion provides the basic substrate for motivating action. This is dictated by evolution and our genetic inheritance. The imperative for the organism is that its neurological state tends towards rewarding feelings. The neuronal circuits that generate feelings can, however, be modulated by higher cognitive activities involving rationality, and the extent to which this happens may well depend on the sheer weight of the neuronal population deployed over time. Cultural training and learning suggest that neocortical activity can reprogram the way experience generates feelings.

Another way of addressing the problem is to ask how a process of reasoning stops. It is a rare event for a conclusive, unassailable answer to be available, and so there has to be another mechanism. This is where rationality has to interact with feeling. The reasoning process stops when the feeling generated by the reasoning is strong enough to make it stop, and that happens when the individual is conscious of the right sort of feeling – a sense of confidence or a subjective certainty of belief. Belief itself can be regarded as a process of reasoning ending with a feeling. The point at which the process stops will vary from person to person, depending on the powers of reasoning brought to bear, but the answer derived is seldom conclusive. If the issue is important enough it is exposed to other minds, and the extended emergent-algorithm is set in train. In reaching an end-point in the reasoning process, populations of neurons will have exerted their role. These populations will almost certainly be grouped into networks, and the nature of the networks themselves may be important, but it is unlikely that we will ever be able to identify them in complex thought processes. We will probably be thrown back on population effects, since even when the process is extended to the social environment, the outcome can be viewed as being related to neuronal populations. Those with greatest neuronal power in the sphere under consideration will have greatest influence. Where there are opposing points of view and resolution is not immediately obvious, the emergent-algorithm will proceed until a consensus dominates – a process that may take many years.

One cautionary note has to be inserted here. In emphasising the possibility of population coding and vector flows being a dominant feature of neuronal activity, it would be wrong to dismiss the importance of computational processes in our mental operations. Vision and language are two areas of brain activity which do seem to have computational aspects, i.e. their processes follow a set of laid-down rules which have to be programmed in particular ways to come up with a result. They do not appear to depend simply on a population vote. It may be that rationality is dependent on the computational powers of the neocortex, but when we come to feelings it is easier to make the case for population coding against computational processes. What could we be computing with feelings? As a crude working hypothesis we might see the *prefrontal cortex-limbic system-autonomic nervous system* network utilising population-coding principles to generate feelings, with the inputs to that domain arising from computational activity in specialised neocortical modules. These modules may well be genetically pre-programmed, but they are almost certainly dependent on sensory experience to become fully functional.

The Opacity of Other Minds

We all know that if we really don't want someone else to know what we are thinking we can easily put up a smoke screen. Actors are trained to portray behaviour which is not accompanied by feelings that usually underlie that behaviour. We can all become actors if we try, and we therefore have to weigh up the possibility that another person might be putting on an act. True, it is difficult to maintain an act in personal life for any length of time, but in transient business relationships it is much easier to act out a role. The success of con men is said to be associated with the image of sincerity they can convey. Although I have no first-hand experience of con men, I have certainly been taken in by people, believing them to be something they weren't. Who hasn't? The naturally devious person is probably at an advantage because they project their own way of thinking on to others, and are on guard against deception. Most people seem to have an instinct to believe what other people say, and that instinct could well be genetically programmed.

Let's have a look at self-awareness from the point of view of one of the folk psychology categories discussed in Chapter 3. I put forward the view that *desires* are often based on feelings and, indeed, can be viewed as a specific variety of feeling. It can often be desire that influences our judgement. The promise of a large reward is generally an inherent part of the scenario for someone being entrapped into an unwise investment, and it can only work if the desire for wealth is present. Admittedly, it is a pretty universal desire, and some are driven by it more strongly than others, but it is a feasible option to make an assessment of how our own particular desires match those of the population immediately around us. Some people talk about their monetary ambitions all the time, others hardly seem to give it a thought. An academic on a professor's salary is hardly likely to be driven by the same financial desires as a speculator in the city, though most academics might welcome a lottery win if it came their way. In the end, though, we have to concede we do not know much about what is going on in the inner recesses of another person's mind regarding their true feelings. We can make a crude estimate based on clues from their words and behaviour, and we can run an 'off-line' simulation as a model in our own mind. But that is subject to large degrees of error because of differing circumstances. Generally speaking, it is bad tactics to project our own values on to someone else, and yet we do it all the time because we have nothing better to work with.

Even if desire is a variety of feeling it must still result from a complex set of neuronal maps. Firstly, there is the memory of what you are desirous of; an image of what you might do with your wealth. How strong a craving does it produce, and what are the symptoms? Do these symptoms include bodily sensations because of activation of the autonomic nervous system? Then you have to analyse the practicality of realising your ambition and what to do about it. Judgements have to be made about how to relate to the community in which the funds are to be raised and with what degree of energy you will pursue your goal. With such a complex interaction of neural states is it any wonder that other people find your mind opaque, and vice versa? We can only piece the evidence together as observable events occur. But that shouldn't stop us forming models of what might be happening – a sort of hypothetico–deductive approach. The important point to remember is that the other person is highly unlikely to have the same complex interactions as yourself.

> It's Frankie's birthday and Johnnie has a strong desire to make her day as special as possible. He never ceases to wonder at the pleasure it gives him to see her all sparkling and bubbly. As a product manager for Mindspace Co. he cannot help wondering about these things. There he is, responsible for the world-wide marketing of rationality, and he gets such pleasure from something so purely irrational. Being self-aware is part of his make-up, and so he is conscious of his desire to please Frankie, which he generally succeeds in doing if he puts his mind to it. They have a splendid meal to celebrate her birthday and Johnnie reflects on the happiness they derive from one another's company. He and Frankie have discussed rationality many times and they agree to differ on its importance in personal life, but Frankie does have a sneaking regard for Johnnie's off-beat definition: Rationality is the ability to recognise when you're being irrational, and to appreciate its charm. She is much less prone to analyse her own desires, and she hasn't had much occasion to worry too much about Johnnie's. They continue to get on exceptionally well together.

Social Interactions

It has been argued that the higher planes of human consciousness have evolved in order to cope with the complexities of social interaction. As a working hypothesis, it has a good deal to commend it. The results of social co-operation are there for everybody to see as the cultures of organisations, companies, and nations evolve or decline. During the course of this exploration I have suggested more than once that the performance of the group may be becoming more important than the interests of the individual as societies battle to hold or improve their position within the global hierarchy. This assertion may provoke a certain amount of lively dissent, so I had better hastily qualify my position. I am only talking about activities where outcomes are dependent on group co-operation. After all, I have acknowledged more than once that we can live our lives on more than one plane. Rationality gives us the power to decide which plane is which.

This reality has to be faced even in the ethereal world of astrophysics, as

Kip Thorne[3] has made plain. He describes the attempt to detect gravitational waves with teams using interferometric detectors:

'The teams were small and intimate, and they worked more or less independently, pursuing their own approaches to the design of interferometric detectors. Within each team the individual scientists had free rein to invent new ideas and pursue them as they wished and for as long as they wished; co-ordination was very loose. This is just the kind of culture that inventive scientists love and thrive on, the culture that Braginsky craves, a culture in which loners like me are happiest. But it is not a culture capable of designing, constructing, debugging and operating large, complex scientific instruments like the several-kilometre-long interferometers required for success.

To design in detail the many complex pieces of such interferometers, to make them all fit together and work together properly, and to keep costs under control and bring the interferometers to completion within a reasonable time, requires a different culture: a culture of tight co-ordination, with subgroups of each team focusing on well-defined tasks and a single director making decisions about what tasks will be done when and by whom.

The road from freewheeling independence to tight co-ordination is a painful one. The world's biology community is traveling that road, with cries of anguish along the way, as it moves towards sequencing the human genome. And we gravitational-wave physicists have been traveling that road since 1984, with no less pain and anguish.'

My own career in the pharmaceutical industry spanned an era when a brilliant biologist, in collaboration with a chemist, could invent a new molecule which could be exploited by their company without taxing its other capabilities to any great extent. Those days have long gone. The technical hurdles which now have to be jumped to get a new medicine on to the market require the same sort of co-ordinated team effort as Kip Thorne describes, though in very different disciplines. We have to add to this the need to grab the attention of a noisy and crowded market-place, which is no less demanding on team effort. The same story will be told time and time again as we are confronted with the demands imposed by a technological age. Does anybody doubt that technology is likely to command the future of economic performance, and that those without the culture to exploit it will be the poor relations?

So, there are social interactions and social interactions. There are those occasions when we are free to indulge our own individuality and those where we have to succumb to the discipline of the group if we want to achieve anything. If you are a writer, a painter, or a composer, there is no great need to conform as long as you can attract an audience or are happy to remain in obscurity. This can be extended to journalists and pop-stars, and many other media activities, where the needs of extended group activity do not necessarily enter into the equation. But these callings are unlikely to determine the economic future. The tune in the post-war decades has been called by the industrial technology of the United States, but many believe that the initiative may now be passing to Far Eastern nations. Japan has already shown what can be done, and Singapore and Hong-Kong have given clear hints of what China might be capable of. In these cultures there are clear limits to which the individual can diverge from the group without experiencing rejection. And yet, I have seen Japanese managers let their hair down at a Geisha party in a way that no staid English businessman would dream of doing in the company of foreign visitors. Once again, it is a question of living on more than one plane.

One of the most memorable experiences I have had on the behaviour of teams was the one I have already referred to at Henley Administrative Staff College, where Meredith Belbin conducted his business games. Personality and intelligence tests were carried out on members of the course before the teams were formed. Belbin used to construct one team which he called 'The Superstars'. The members of this team had achieved some of the top scores on creativity and analytical ability, and Belbin was always right in his prediction of their performance in the business game. They would not win. The reason he was so sure of his prediction was that the team members could be relied on not to agree with one another about the best course of action. Their egos got in the way. A spirit of co-operative subordination to the team interest and the ability to empathise with others was not their forte. Consciousness of the requirements of effective group action is as precious a commodity as being intelligent and energetic, and it could be characterised as a form of group rationality.

Interaction with others and the ability to interpret their disposition is, of course, not confined to teams, but for our purposes we need to avoid too deep an analysis of relationships such as Frankie and Johnnie's. Here, there are sparse grounds for rational evaluation, except for that involved in individuals applying it to their own self-awareness. We could, with sufficient imagination, create a distribution curve of interactions, ranging from those which involve no more than some personal aspect of the lives of the individuals concerned, to those which involve affairs of state and the fate of nations. One word would be sufficient to conjure up a scene at the 'broad affairs' end of the curve – Munich. This one word illustrates the power of language to trigger thoughts which are not explicit in the nature of the word or phrase employed, but which have an ability to evoke mental imagery because of background learning and memory. It would be inappropriate to try and analyse the encounter between Neville Chamberlain and Adolf Hitler in terms of their mental attributes and neural architecture because we have insufficient information, but it might be easier to do this than analyse a job interview between Stalin and a potential replacement for Beria! This may seem unduly frivolous, but the point should be apparent in a minute.

A better illustration of high stakes in the modern world would be an economic summit, with the health of the global economy at stake. Without resorting to a scenario of war, which can hardly be presented as a model of rational behaviour, this probably presents as hideously complex a challenge to the mind and nervous system of modern man as it is possible to devise, because all the ingredients are there: uncertainty, highly involved matters, cross-cultural exchanges, personal reputations at stake, the economic fate of millions, and CNN television cameras to convey any slip to the world. The leaders enter the meeting room and exchange friendly banter, at the same time assessing whether they are talking to a potential ally or an opponent. As political figures they have robust nervous systems, hardened by a lifetime of political rough and tumble. Like all of us, they do have autonomic nervous systems which tend to become activated during moments of stress, but they are adept at masking and controlling their symptoms. You are the leader of a country which is likely to come under attack for its trade practices, and you will be pressed for concessions which will undermine your status back home if they are conceded. You suspect you have several other states lined up against you. Your aids and advisers are clearly nervous and are giving you all sorts of gratuitous advice, but it is you who has to perform in the arena with the other gladiators. What precious gift of mind would be most valuable to you at this moment? First on *my* list would be the power to get inside the other minds present, which language, cultural differences and deliberate deception can make extraordinarily opaque. And yet, the egos around the table probably do not give much attention to this aspect of the interchange, obsessed as they are with the demands of the subject and the output of their own neural circuits. How did Chamberlain manage to misread Hitler, and how did Roosevelt deceive himself about Stalin? My guess would be – projecting their own values.

We all do it, and in a sense it is inevitable. On what other basis are we able to make an assessment? We have no direct experience of mental phenomenology except that occurring in our own minds. But, with a little determination, we can make an effort to rise above our own conscious and unconscious assumptions and attempt to assess the field of possibilities. This entails acceptance of the probability that the other person will have radically different beliefs and feelings to our own, so that we deliberately look for diagnostic signs in statements and questions. Those who are socially skilled are able intuitively to decipher signals to a remarkable degree. On the other hand, we have seen that individuals suffering from autistic syndromes have a marked lack of ability to project themselves into another person's mind, and this produces social problems for them. They can be thought of as lying at one end of the distribution curve of mind-reading talent. How would you rate yourself as a mind-reader? It may be that you have an unconscious processor in your brain which generally gives you a reliable answer about where others are coming from, or it may be that only occasionally does chance throw up circumstances where your own intuitive approach dovetails in with the disposition of others. The way we assess our own beliefs, desires and feelings will have a large measure of influence on the way we apply rational analysis to another's attitudes.

It is conceivable that consciousness as an agent of social action could go in one of many directions, and there are hordes of dedicated activists who will try to press it in their preferred direction. It seems hardly likely that the blind forces of natural selection will have any role in determining the outcome, but cultural selection may be a different matter, even though it is extraordinarily difficult to discern trends in the maelstrom of confusing activity that we see around the world. The question for consciousness is whether it will remain self-centred, primarily concerned with beliefs, desires, feelings and thoughts of the individual, or whether it will reach out towards a greater understanding of others, developing mutual empathy within the group through self-awareness. In some of the earlier parts of this account I have referred to trends which give cause for pessimism, but we have to recognise that the media selectively distorts the picture of how people behave, always looking for the dramatic or the outrageous while most of the world goes quietly about its business. Although it must be true that the media can have a conditioning influence on minds as it bombards people with the same sort of emotionally charged stuff day-in day-out, we have to recognise it has to look after its own survival and it purveys what experience shows will generate an audience. But we should not overate its influence. In the end it is achievement which counts rather than any side-line commentary on life. Like it or not, there has to be a strong chance that technological activities will call the shots if they generate economic success.

During the course of my career in the pharmaceutical industry I saw quite remarkable changes, both in technology and the organisational style needed to manage it. I feel pretty confident this experience has been repeated widely within other industries, and not just manufacturing industry. You only have to experience the massive co-ordination and teamwork which is required in the airline industry, and the way the banks work, to appreciate that. Is all this dehumanising? Not one bit, would be my conclusion, and, in fact, you could argue quite the opposite. The more we develop our powers to understand others, the greater the chance that humankind will develop a society that eliminates the outrageous and destructive bursts of the irrational ego, group or otherwise. This should not inhibit us from pursuing the highest forms of aesthetic and cultural enjoyment at the individual level.

Chapter 8

Consciousness, Self, and Society

Some Puzzles of Consciousness

The hunt for the neural correlate of consciousness is well underway, but it is not at all certain that this research programme will get to the bottom of the most fundamental property of the human mind. Although we all have a good idea of what consciousness is, it is difficult to define and there are a host of theories about its nature. Philosophical ideas tend to concentrate on the subjective or *phenomenal* aspects of consciousness, elements that give rise to what philosophers refer to as *qualia*. An example of a quale (singular of qualia) is the redness of red. Colour does not actually exist in the universe, only electromagnetic radiation. It is the brain which interprets a 700 nm wavelength of visible light as red, and there is no way to determine whether the subjective sensation of red in one person is the same as that experienced by another.

The *sensations* we have seem to be at the heart of consciousness, and they can be bodily sensations like pain as well as the result of perceptions of the external world. At the present time it is impossible to say how subjective sensations (qualia) arise in purely physical beings since these qualia do not have a physical presence which is amenable to measurement. Even if we could identify the neural correlate of a particular sensation, we would still be unable to say how that neural configuration gave rise to the experience of the sensation. It is resolution of this aspect of consciousness that some philosophers believe to be beyond the intellectual capacities of mankind. We will return to this intractable issue shortly, but first it would be worthwhile to consider features of the brain which are known to be associated with consciousness.

Only certain parts of the brain are absolutely essential for consciousness. No animal remains conscious after bilateral ablation of the thalamus. Large tracts of the neocortex can be removed without producing unconsciousness, though of course the nature of consciousness is altered. Damage to the occipital lobes causes blindness, and profound changes can occur if other areas of the sensory cortex are injured, as the examples given in Chapter 1 indicate. Removal of the hippocampus and related nuclei causes severe memory defects, and if the amygdala is damaged there are changes in emotional response; but consciousness remains. The thalamus plays an

essential role in establishing consciousness, but this doesn't say anything
about content, and the most intriguing question about consciousness is its
content – the images, words and feelings that we experience in our minds.
Nuclei in the thalamus, along with the reticular formation in the mid-brain,
are together sometimes referred to as the *extended reticular–thalamic
activating system* (ERTAS)[1], and if this system acts as the all important
power source for the brain it still leaves the important question of what is
activated when it is switched on. There is wide agreement that the content
of consciousness depends on the neocortex.

We have already seen that the thalamus is the receiving station for all
sensory inputs into the brain, apart from olfaction, and that descending
pathways from the cortex outnumber ascending pathways by a considerable
multiple (four to one is a favoured estimate). There is extensive two-way
signalling between thalamus and cortex, and between the thalamus and
other subcortical structures. Animals other than human beings experience
consciousness, though they have a much less well developed neocortex, or
none at all. The higher cognitive processes that we humans enjoy are
probably not shared by other animals, and they certainly do not have the
benefit of language. A human infant has more neurons and synapses than an
adult, but it has not yet established the memory circuits and language
capability in its neocortex. When only a few weeks' old, it has not even
learned to see and hear properly, but it is, nevertheless, still conscious. A
baby will respond in no uncertain manner to any discomfort in its internal
bodily state. This should make it clear why it is so difficult to define
consciousness, but a minimum criterion would seem to be that the organism
should be conscious *of* something – that is, there has to be *intentionality*.

Intentionality is a peculiarly philosophical word which is not met in
normal discourse and it refers to the fact that consciousness has to be
directed at something; has to be about something. Even this might be
challenged by people of a mystical persuasion who believe that, through a
process of meditation, they can achieve 'pure' consciousness, empty of any
content. This is a difficult matter to resolve since we only have the word of
the subjects for their experience, and it may be they simply lose consciousness for a while, or their memory of it. If they are able to report anything at
all there must be content of some sort, even if it is only a mystical *feeling*.
In certain types of epilepsy, patients experience momentary loss of contact
with their surroundings, though the individual may still be able to perform
movement. Is there actual loss of consciousness, or is memory simply lost
for that short period? There are anaesthetic agents used in surgical procedures which allow the patient to respond to commands during the
operation, but the patient has no recollection of the procedure, or any pain

or discomfort, afterwards. Can something be called a conscious experience if there is no memory of it seconds afterwards? Perhaps the debate around these fine points of consciousness will eventually produce an important insight, but for a working understanding of consciousness we need to look at more widely shared experiences.

There are plenty of theories about consciousness, but none of them has taken hold on a wide scale, let alone on a universal scale like Darwin's theory of evolution. The reason for this is lack of evidence. One of the existing theories might be on the right track, but the time is not yet ripe for its recognition. Where will the evidence come from? The creation of artificial consciousness would certainly help to resolve matters, but there is no sign of that on the horizon. It is unlikely that philosophy can ever provide the answer because it is not a primary generator of evidence; some kind of scientific endeavour has to be involved for that. But the difficulty that neuroscience faces is obvious, even supposing it could develop the capability of monitoring individual neurons and their circuits by non-invasive techniques. In such circumstances I might offer myself for investigation with a challenge to the investigators that they identify what is happening in my mind during a moment of consciousness. They should be able to see a large number of neurons firing (hopefully), but the chances of their identifying a particular thought associated with that activity and what-it-is-like to have the thought, are virtually non-existent. They would have to ask me to find out. True, they could then repeat the experiment and undertake some statistical correlations between sequential measurements of neuronal patterns and their relationship to thoughts and feelings, but they would always be dependent on my subjective reports. Neuroscientist Walter Freeman has worked for many years on the olfactory system in rabbits, monitoring hundreds of thousands of neurons, and has found no repeatable patterns even for a simple sniff. The spatial patterns generated in the rabbit's olfactory bulb change every time and appear to depend on past experience. The nature of each moment is influenced by a previous moment, and can only be interpreted by the animal concerned.

It is legitimate to ask whether consciousness is dependent on neuronal firing patterns or whether more fundamental forces are at work. Quantum coherence in the microtubules of neurons has been put forward as a possible candidate[2], and the idea that quantum states may be significant in conscious experience is supported by a number of physicists because the outcome of measurements in quantum mechanics is affected by the conscious observer. This leads to the interesting question of whether an individual neuron can be conscious, or whether there is a minimum number of neurons required for consciousness. There are plenty of neurons firing in our central and peripheral nervous systems which never contribute to consciousness, and so we are still left wondering what particular configuration of neurons leads to a conscious event. Another possibility is that consciousness is a fundamental property of the universe and cannot be reduced to the activity of neurons or subneuronal structures, but, if so, it is a strange coincidence that consciousness has only been observed in conjunction with assemblies of neurons. These are interesting concepts on which to speculate but they cannot lead anywhere unless there is evidence, and that is completely lacking at the present time.

The one conclusion that observable facts lead us towards with confidence is that consciousness is associated with nervous systems, and these appear only in the biological systems of animals. Plants do not have nervous systems and there is no evidence that they have developed any form of consciousness. How are we to judge at what level consciousness appears in animals with primitive nervous systems? Does purposeful movement signify consciousness, and, if so, is an earthworm conscious? Anyone who has tried to swat a fly can be in no doubt that it has a sensory system which allows it to avoid all but the swiftest and deadliest of aims, so does it become 'conscious' of the impending blow? Memory associated with protein synthesis at nerve synapses has been demonstrated in the most lowly of creatures (sea slug and fruit fly), but is memory a fundamental qualification for consciousness? Although we are unable to define consciousness in a satisfactory manner, we can conclude that it arose in its earliest manifestation at a stage in the evolutionary process before the high-powered circuitry of the human neocortex had developed. If we confine ourselves to human beings to examine consciousness, the aspect we are most interested in is that associated with the higher order neocortical activity which gives us our integrated awareness of the world and an appreciation of our inner states. One could hardly attribute such concepts to a fly.

The Prefrontal Cortex

One of the most interesting areas for examining aspects of high-order human consciousness is that part of the brain credited with housing the most evolutionarily advanced part of the neocortex – the frontal lobes. We have already seen from earlier chapters that the frontal cortex has a crucial role in working memory[3] and in enabling us to formulate our plans. It is, in particular, the neocortex of the prefrontal regions which appears to control important functions in the brain associated with sound judgement and rational behaviour. The best evidence for this emerges from patients who have sustained damage to their prefrontal cortex and who exhibit clear deficits in managing their lives. Many parallel divisions of activity are packed into the prefrontal cortex, so it would be wrong to regard it as having a single, central area of executive operations, but for our purposes we can consider its collection of multiple, special purpose systems as operating within a unit.

The real importance of prefrontal activity becomes apparent when considering *off-line simulation.* You will recall this expression arose in describing mental processes we employ to judge responses of other minds and when considering problems that do not immediately confront us. Responses to external stimuli in the here-and-now can be thought of as on-line. Research has suggested that humans spend much of their time thinking off-line[4] and that this activity becomes seriously impaired if there is damage to the prefrontal cortex. In order to think off-line we have to create models in our minds and call upon our memories. The prefrontal cortex controls the *working memory* which is necessary to forage effectively through memory banks in the sensory cortex and so come up with images and ideas. We then select the ideas we think are most realistic by judging them against our perception of the external world. In going through this kind of thought process we normally consider a number of options for action, rejecting those which we *feel* are least likely to produce the desired outcome. This is where the prefrontal cortex has to interact with the limbic system and other subcortical structures in judging the balance between rational and emotional factors.

It might help to make things clearer by considering the important role of fantasy as an off-line activity. Although we cannot make dogmatic statements about other minds it is a fair assumption that we all fantasise from time to time and examine possible scenarios we may be involved in. Winning the national lottery, writing a best seller, or having dinner with a famous personality are possibilities we may consider, but we realise the probability of any such occurrence is very small. We then go on to downgrade our expectations and consider more plausible scenarios. There is a whole scale of possibilities we can run through and we have to match those possibilities against our track record and an assessment of our ability, determination and luck. If we are of a pessimistic frame of mind we might start our fantastic journey at the other end of the spectrum, as some people do when they have a feeling of impending disaster. A reality check may show that this frame of thinking is also inappropriate. But unless we go through an elimination routine of this sort it is difficult to establish goals, and that is what patients with prefrontal damage find so hard to do. It is also worth noting that, as far as we know, humans are the only species that can undertake such off-line analysis. A chimpanzee can hardly wake up in the forest and think 'what shall I do today?', because it doesn't have the linguistic concept to do so. Activity during the day is probably determined by a series of on-line stimuli, both internal and external.

The concept of consciousness most useful to us, then, centres on activity which produces an awareness of the world around us against the background knowledge we have of ourselves and our mental processes. We can look back at events that have occurred in the past and think how circumstances might have been different had we played things differently. In psychological jargon this is known as evaluating *counterfactuals*. With such simulations we can avoid making the same mistakes over and over again. If we are unable to employ the prefrontal cortex to run an historical review of this kind we will have difficulty in planning our future actions. Even though we may have a fully operational prefrontal cortex, the way we employ it is going to depend on the circuits that have developed and the competition that occurs between neuronal populations. Investigations in split-brain patients (where the corpus callosum has been severed) have shown up significant differences between right and left hemispheres, apart from the obvious one of language. Michael Gazzaniga[5] sees the dominant left hemisphere as the major force in our cognitive lives, and he has characterised it as 'the interpreter' which moulds our beliefs. Others, like Philip Johnson-Laird[6], regard mental *models*, rather than language, as the natural way in which the mind constructs reality, and give the right hemisphere the most significant role in reasoning. So now, we not only have prefrontal, but perhaps prefrontal left and right! The problem in evaluating the evidence is that it arises in radically different ways. The Gazzaniga evidence results from experience with split-brain patients, and that cited by Johnson-Laird from unilateral anterior temporal lobectomy. Both procedures obviously upset the normal balance of the brain and further studies will be necessary to sort out left brain, right brain differences.

The Emergent-Algorithm

I introduced the concept of the emergent-algorithm in the Introduction, using the establishment of historical reputations to illustrate the idea. Society is not a closed, self-sustaining energy system like an organism, but it still manages to express its experience in an accessible manner if suitable techniques are employed. These may involve statistically based opinion surveys, when we end up with what might be described as a measure of the 'attractor state' on the issue – the observable outcome of the myriad events which form the historical process and society's assessment of it. The functioning of the individual human brain has obvious differences to the functioning of society. For a start, it is a closed, isolated system which can only be assessed by a third party through observation of conscious behaviour, though once again verbal and body language can be thought of as constituting the attractor state for the organism. We can develop a model of how this might work.

The first requirement is that the brain has to be switched on. ERTAS (the extended reticular–thalamic activating system) looks like the favourite candidate for this role. Its energising effect will differ in degree from individual to individual. The extent of its action will depend on neurotransmitter profiles in crucial nuclei, and the underlying metabolism within neurons. Rhythmic patterns of neuronal firing may be important. Various areas of the neocortex become activated either by external sensory stimuli or by internally generated thoughts. The complexity of this activity is immense, involving populations of neurons and their networks throughout the brain. We have little chance of identifying exactly what is happening at the micro-level but we can apportion macro-activity. Search and evaluation is probably orchestrated by the prefrontal cortex, but memories and conceptual models which have to be manipulated will be distributed throughout the sensory cortex. It is likely that numerous embryonic proto-thoughts spring up as neuronal events, many of which are rejected in favour of other thoughts which start to take a significant place within consciousness. This could well be a population effect relying on the weight of neuronal patterns. As an analogy, think of events in society competing for historical importance. Most of them fall by the wayside. It takes time for the significance of events to become apparent, and in the end it is a decision of the informed population. Our brains work on a much shorter timescale, but we know it takes time for us to sort out our thoughts. Something which seems a good idea at first may be dropped for a much sounder alternative after due reflection. How do we know when to stop our cognitive activities and make a decision? For that we have to rely on our emotional centres and the feelings they generate, so the computations in our neocortex have to be linked into subcortical systems. We do not always come up with the best answer for ourselves, but society will make a statistical judgement on our decisions over time, and we flourish if the verdict is favourable more often than not. Subcortex, sensory cortex and frontal cortex have all played their vital roles in producing a conscious act.

Even if the things we are conscious of result from an algorithmic process, it still leaves a puzzle at both ends of the process. Supposing we knew how proto-thoughts and memories were encoded at the local level of neural populations and networks and how the resultant winning-thought could be identified at the global level, we would still not know how they presented themselves as conscious experiences in the mind. It raises the question of whether there is a fundamental aspect of energy patterns which science is unaware of at the present time. Everything in the universe seems to be related to energy of one kind or another, even time and space, but there is no evidence that consciousness appears in anything but animal nervous systems.

Whether or not consciousness is the result of an emergent-algorithm it is a safe bet that rationality is, as we troll through arguments, models and evidence to reach our conclusions. Representational systems have to be used that need serial processing, even if massive parallel activity is going on underneath conscious awareness. Clearly, consciousness exists at levels much lower than the neuronal complexity required for rationality, and the best exemplars of that in man are sensations and feelings. Even these are mightily complex. If consciousness is in any way fundamental there must be a common thread running right through its various manifestations. If only we could define its first appearance!

Chapter 9

Frankie and Johnnie Discuss Consciousness and Rationality

Frankie put down the manuscript she was reading and smiled at Johnnie. 'Not a bad effort, but like everyone else you get on to consciousness in the end. I thought you were supposed to be promoting rationality.'

'I am, but you can hardly ignore consciousness in tackling rationality', Johnnie countered, rather defensively.

'True; but if you're going to end on the theme of consciousness don't you think you ought to adopt a more fundamental approach? After all, it's you who are so fond of emergent-algorithms.'

'I'm not sure what you mean.'

'Why not look at things more from the perspective of physics?', suggested Frankie.

'I'm a biologist, not a mathematician,' countered Johnnie, 'and besides, I think quantum mechanics is the wrong level at which to look at consciousness.'

'I'm aware of that, but you can hardly say that energy is irrelevant. You cannot have emergent-algorithms without energy, so you should consider its fundamental nature. You've read Steven Weinberg's *The First Three Minutes*. According to him the universe more or less started off as pure energy, with elementary particles being created and annihilated, then created again as the temperature cooled. This must have been the first emergent-algorithm.'

'It may have been,' conceded Johnnie, 'but it's a long way removed from consciousness.'

'I wonder,' mused Frankie. 'It was your passing comment about "energy and time" in the last chapter which prompted the thought. It made me think about electromagnetism and why it is that the speed of light is a constant around which everything else has to revolve – space, time and mass. Why should that be?'

'Search me; but I don't see what it has got to do with consciousness, because brains don't operate at the speed of light. It might be more relevant to computers.'

'Okay. But if we accept $E = mc^2$ we can eventually relate everything to electromagnetic energy. Suppose we take up your idea of the emergent-algorithm and think of applying this to energy. If there were no energy there would be no time or space. It is the emergent-algorithm of energy which creates time and space for any observer not operating at the speed of light. For a photon, time and space mean nothing. It wouldn't understand all this business about quantum non-locality and collapse of the wave function because time and space don't exist for it. It is only because we are sub-light-speed observers with consciousness that we get puzzled by it all.'

'Interesting idea,' conceded Johnnie, whose structural sense could partially overcome his rudimentary grasp of theoretical physics, even of the amateur Frankie variety. 'We're a bit out of our depth in discussing space/time, but I suppose if energy has been condensed into matter since the Big-Bang, gravity could be a remnant effect of electromagnetism associated with matter and space. Perhaps the fact that gravitational waves have not yet been detected is to do with their enormous wavelength and low energy level.'

'Let's not get side-tracked on to gravity,' suggested Frankie, 'but consider the main sequence of events in the emergent-algorithm of the universe. Energy condensed into matter and then, eventually, energy interacted with matter to create life. After a decent interval, life gave rise to consciousness, and to do so it had to utilise energy in a specialised way. The interesting question is, what comes after consciousness?'

'An intriguing thought, but let's just dwell on life and consciousness for a moment. There does seem to be this connection between consciousness in animals and the capacity for movement, which we can think of as a form of kinetic energy, but it is difficult to see the more highly evolved forms of consciousness involving thought and rationality having any relationship to movement.'

'Agreed. We know that energy can neither be created nor destroyed, but the second law of thermodynamics does imply that the amount of usable energy decreases in any closed system. If we consider the universe as a closed system it means eventual heat death, unless there is a way round the problem. Nuclear fusion is one way of regenerating energy from matter, but life also has the ability to recycle matter and release energy. Consciousness itself is a significant utiliser of energy and the only way animal life has been able to generate the required energy is to utilise organic matter in the form of edible material. It would take a better mathematician than me, though, to work out the net balance of forces.'

'If energy is the basis for life, which it obviously is,' Johnny asserted confidently, 'it is amazing how it has generated such intricate processes in biological systems. They defeat detailed description by any mathematical approach that mankind has developed, or is likely to develop.'

'That's undoubtedly true, since all mathematics can do is describe statistical relationships in energy systems. As you mentioned in your manuscript, it would be a hopeless task to try and follow the detail of emergent-algorithms in any complex system. We know that the non-linear behaviour of chaotic systems defeats that objective. This could prevent us penetrating the system surrounding consciousness.'

'Perhaps, but we should be able to develop more insight than we have now. The interesting puzzle about consciousness is that, although it is clearly dependent on energy, there seems to be no way of tapping its output apart from the experience of the subject concerned. This is why it is so difficult to get away from some version of dual aspect theory – that there is another side of the coin to the functional activity of neurons.'

'Yes,' agreed Frankie, 'how *does* the subjective element of consciousness express itself? My guess is that it has to be some kind of statistical effect.'

'There is plenty of evidence that human consciousness needs a finite time to express itself, somewhere between 50 milliseconds and 500 milliseconds. Specific modules in the brain need to be involved, though not the same ones all the time, apart from ERTAS. There is obviously spatial distribution of activity, presumably involving some aspect of energy that we are as yet unaware of. And why should that activity only be manifest in nervous systems? My guess is that the nature of memory is an essential ingredient in the process.'

'Well, we could combine both hunches,' suggested Frankie, 'and think about statistical patterns of memory, whether inherited genetically or laid down through learning.'

'I often think about Shakespeare,' said Johnnie, leaving Frankie groping momentarily for the connection. 'There is a statistical view of his genius within society, both inherited through expressed values and learned directly from reading his works. Does society have a "consciousness" about Shakespeare other than that detectable through individual opinions? He is an interesting example because the emergent-algorithm of his reputation is so widely and firmly established.'

'If a visitor arrived from outer space with the technology to monitor all human activity it would be able to detect activities which established the significance of Shakespeare in the English-speaking world, without requiring subjective reports. But that still leaves us with the problem of the observer, and we know the brain has no observer.'

'So, somehow a system of global monitoring of events in the brain has to come up with a conclusion, without an observer. The Damasios believe that it can be achieved by perturbations in the self-system.'

'That sounds a bit mysterious to me,' interjected Frankie.

'Well, you will recall my point about how the process of rational thought stops. It cannot do it because it comes up with the right answer, because there is seldom any right answer. But it can generate a feeling that there is a right thing to do. The individual has a visceral sense about the best way forward, which involves the autonomic nervous system and its somatic feedback as well as various centres in the subcortex.'

'I'm not so sure about that,' said Frankie. 'I'm not aware of any particular feeling when I am checking the accounts and I come up with the conclusion that they are correct. That is a purely rational process'.

'Hmm,' reflected Johnnie. 'That sounds fine, but you know that the figures in the accounts are only approximations of the real situation, and many of them are wild guesses. I know because I submit some of them. How do you decide whether or not to believe the figures you're dealing with?'

'I take you're point. For the figures themselves I have to rely on the integrity of the system and the checks we run, but I am really talking about the internal consistency of the figures in the accounts. You can check those on a rational basis. A mathematician knows whether the solution he has derived for a problem is logically correct.'

'I suppose I have to concede that there are some logical systems where a correct answer can be derived, but it represents a very limited corner of human activity and it must be debatable whether you actually need consciousness for such activity. Just employ a computer. Most of us are concerned with the future and what to do about it. In anything you deal with which contains a forecast you have to decide whether to believe it or not, and that means deciding whether there is a reasonable level of probability that the forecast will prove accurate, and with what tolerance. Forecasts are never spot on.'

'I appreciate you thinking of me as a computer,' chided Frankie. 'I suppose that's why we accountants are all so boring.'

'I thought I was the boring one,' Johnnie said in conciliatory tone. 'And if we look at our life together it's you who makes the decision on most of our activities – what we eat and how we furnish the flat. How much logic do you use for that?'

'Well, I do take into consideration what you might think, and there is a certain rationality in that.'

'Maybe, but in the end its feelings that count.'

'Yes, but even if I concede that feelings are important, which of course I do, you still haven't overcome the problem of how they manifest themselves subjectively.'

At that moment Radar the cat sprang on to Frankie's lap, and nuzzled up against her. 'What about Radar here?,' she said. 'He must be feeling something.'

'He must be conscious of the fact that he can get some reward by jumping on to your lap, but his consciousness could be confined to a level of feeling. If you were not sitting in the room in front of him it is unlikely he would be thinking, 'I can't wait until she gets home so that I can jump on her lap'. Off-line thinking is not a speciality of cats, especially in the feelings department.'

'Don't insult poor Radar,' Frankie cooed, stroking the cat and temporarily losing interest in the conversation.

'There are plenty of people who agree with Antonio Damasio about feelings,' Johnnie persisted, 'but you could hardly describe it as a consensus because opinion on consciousness is so fragmented. You can see this in the plethora of books on the subject and in the on-line Internet forums.'

'Are you just trying to add to the confusion then?' quipped Frankie.

'Almost all the thinking on the subject takes place in the academic stratosphere, and I'm just trying to bring it down to earth. What use is rationality if it's confined to a few who don't influence events to any great extent? There has to be mass movement on the issue if it's to get anywhere.'

'One minute you're saying it's feelings that are important, and the next minute rationality. You even confuse me, let alone anyone reading your book, if they ever do!'

'The point I am trying to make is that the two are inseparable and act in concert. I believe we should train people to understand how these two aspects of mind interact, even if it is only the first step in a thousand mile journey. At the moment there isn't even widespread acknowledgement of the problem. My contention is that we are only going to get the evidence we need from population studies, and that has to be statistical in nature.'

'Give me a simple picture, then,' challenged Frankie.

'We have to start with our emotional system, because that's the one we inherited in the emergent-algorithm of evolution. As important as our sensory systems are, and of course we also inherited those, I would like to put them to one side in terms of the neocortical computations that are involved. There is sufficient empirical evidence that our senses function pretty reliably for the majority of the population. It is the emotional reactions that perceptions produce which really differentiate people from one another; responses depending on genetic inheritance, formative experience, and the memory systems that these have laid down. The importance of the early years cannot be overstressed. I find it astounding that there is evidence that infants start to lose the ability to discriminate sounds in non-native languages between the ages of 10 to 12 months.'

'In that case you should give up your French lessons,' interjected Frankie.

Johnnie ignored the remark. 'Our emotional system modulates virtually all our sensory activity, and it is a different variation on a theme for each of us. We may all have similar neural architecture but the way it functions has been determined by many years of individual experience and its interaction with the relevant genes we have inherited. Subcortical structures are at the heart of emotion, and I think it's fair to regard the thalamus as the integrating centre, even though the limbic system has a crucial role. The link between subcortex and body is important for our being aware of the state of our feelings. We know that if we dampen down autonomic nervous activity we can influence mental outlook and mood. The effect that strong emotional reactions, like love and hate, can have is obvious but I am concerned with the more subtle role of every-day feelings. Even when you're doing the accounts you have to make assessments about the accuracy of data, and feelings come into it. You're either happy with the estimates on plant costs, or you're not, and the deadlines you have to meet can leave you flustered and concerned. I know, I've seen it.'

'All right Mr Automaton, you're not giving me any great insight into myself' said Frankie, as she threw Radar onto the floor.

'I know that,' conceded Johnnie, 'but you can see how the most innocent remark produces an emotional response. It is inescapable, but what is often absent is an analysis of that response. We have both become accustomed to barbed remarks from one another, and we can easily place them in context, but if they came from your boss they could leave you uncertain about his attitude. Was he joking and just being awkwardly sociable, or did he mean to give you a real dig?'

'I have less trouble with my boss than with you,' pouted Frankie, 'you have a real insensitivity about some of the things you say.'

'I'm sorry about that. I accept my tongue-in-cheek remarks can be mis-construed, but you have to realise I say things lightly. It's deeds not words that count in my book.'

'I know. But I think you're in danger of losing the point you were making.'

'Thank you. If we can agree that feelings arise from the smallest incidents we have to decide how we deal with them. Do we simply ride with them and react accordingly or subject them to rational analysis? I suggest the latter is beneficial in any group activity with a specific object-ive, and so we have to bring the prefrontal cortex into play. This enables us to assess ourselves in the context of the group and to plan an effective strategy. The ability to make good judgements in managing their lives appears to be absent in patients with prefrontal damage. If feelings are wandering about all the time or are relatively inactive, it makes it difficult to stick with firm intentions.'

'That seems to be an oversimplification to me,' Frankie interjected. 'I accept that the frontal lobes are important; they must have developed to the size they are in man for a reason; but how do they set about exerting their rationality? Doesn't left-brain language or right-brain modelling count? I don't see how you can ascribe rationality to the prefrontal cortex without involving functions in the rest of the brain.'

'Absolutely,' Johnnie responded enthusiastically. 'The trouble with describing anything in the brain, because it is so massively parallel, is that we are confined by the serial nature of language to saying one thing at a time. It cannot be said too often that conscious activity probably requires global processing in the brain, but something has to probe and select contributions from the different modules. This is probably an activity of the prefrontal cortex because we know it has an important role in working memory. How the unity of awareness is achieved, we don't know. If we could solve that we would probably be 90% of the way towards solving consciousness.'

'Sounds plausible. But, as you keep saying yourself, what we need is evidence. How on earth are we going to get that?'

'That's the difficult part. My own feeling is that designer brains will be a long time coming, if they ever come at all, and we have to look for population effects which give us statistical confidence in our assertions. It's no use confining studies to totally artificial situations because they can only scratch the surface. That would be like assessing a new drug on its animal pharmacology without carrying out clinical trials. My guess is that careful study of psycho-active drugs in large populations will produce insights. Most current agents are hopelessly unselective in their activity, but biotechnology will provide agents with more specific modes of action. Proteins probably. The problem will be getting them into the brain, and it will be unethical to do so unless there is a good therapeutic reason. So, we will depend on a combination of neuropsychology and therapeutic intervention in a controlled manner.'

'What about neuroscience,' Frankie queried, 'surely that's going to provide useful insights?'

'Of course,' Johnnie replied, 'but I doubt that it's going to do much to solve aspects of higher-order consciousness, like the rationality/emotionality equation. That can only be achieved in human beings, and the neural circuits involved are so complex that we will be forced to rely on statistical measurements. If we were going to solve consciousness with sensory measurements we should be nearly home by now.'

'I'm aware it's time for a drink,' said Frankie, bringing them down to earth. 'Would you like a glass of wine or an orange juice?'

'A glass of wine, I think,' Johnnie responded. 'It's time I scrambled some of these neuronal circuits, otherwise they might go into spasm. Interesting how well the brain has coped with alcohol over the centuries. As a simple molecule I suppose it acts similarly to anaesthetics in binding to membrane proteins, and in modest amounts its actions are entirely reversible. Why should we feel such benefit from the dulling of our sharper faculties? It illustrates the uneasy relationship between our higher centres and our feeling-self. But I feel very good at the moment. Come here!'

And there rational discussion ended.

References

Introduction

1. Carruthers, P., and Smith P. K. (1996). *Theories of Theories of Mind.* Cambridge: Cambridge University Press.
2. Baron-Cohen, S. (1995). *Mindblindness.* Cambridge, MA: Bradford Books, MIT Press.
3. Jones, S. (1993). *The Language of Genes.* London: Harper Collins.
4. McGinn, C. (1991). *The Problem of Consciousness.* Oxford: Blackwell.
5. Penrose, R. (1989). *The Emperor's New Mind.* Oxford: Oxford University Press.
6. Kauffmann, S. (1995). *At Home in the Universe.* London: Viking, Penguin Books.

Chapter 1: Some Insights into the Brain

1. Macdonald, C., and Macdonald, G. (1995). *Connectionism.* Oxford: Blackwell.
2. Hebb, D. O. (1949). *Organisation of Behaviour.* New York: Wiley.
3. Hardcastle. V. G. (1995). *Locating Consciousness.* Amsterdam: John Benjamins.
4. Hebb, D. O. (1980). *Essay on Mind.* Hillsdale, NJ: Lawrence Erlbaum Assocs.
5. Edelman, G. (1992). *Bright Air, Brilliant Fire.* London: Allen Lane, Penguin Books.
6. Luria, A. R. (1987). *The Man with a Shattered World.* Cambridge, MA: Havard University Press.
7. Sacks, O. (1985). *The Man Who Mistook his Wife for a Hat.* London: Picador, Pan Books.
8. Schacter, D. L., and Tulving, E. (1994). *Memory Systems 1994.* Cambridge, MA: Bradford Books, MIT Press.

Chapter 2: Observations on Mental Repertoires

1. Mayr, E. (1982). *The Growth of Biological Thought.* Cambridge, MA: Havard University Press.
2. Sutherland, S. (1992). *Irrationality: The Enemy Within.* London: Constable & Co. Ltd.
3. Herrnstein, R. J., and Murray, C. (1994). *The Bell Curve.* New York, NY: Simon and Schuster Inc.

Chapter 3: A Deeper Excursion into Folk Psychology

1. Dunbar, S. (1995). *The Trouble with Science*. London: Faber & Faber Ltd.
2. Ridley, M. (1996). *The Origins of Virtue*. London: Penguin Books Ltd.
3. Gazzaniga, M. S. (1992). *Nature's Mind*. New York, NY: Harper-Collins.
4. Damasio, A. R. (1994). *Descartes' Error*. New York, NY: Grosset/Putnam.
5. Gregory, L. R. (Ed.). (1987). *The Oxford Companion to the Mind*. Oxford: Oxford University Press.
6. Hobson, T. A. (1994). *The Chemistry of Conscious States*. New York, NY: Little, Brown & Company.

Chapter 4: Factors Influencing Thought

1. Dennett, D. C. (1991). *Consciousness Explained*. New York, NY: Little, Brown & Co.
2. Churchland, P. S., and Sejnowski, T. J. (1992). *The Computational Brain*. Cambridge, MA: MIT Press.
3. Broadbent, D. E. (1958). *Perception and Communication*. Oxford: Pergamon.
4. Sass, L. A. (1992). *Madness and Modernism*. New York, NY: Harper-Collins.
5. Crick, F. (1994). *The Astonishing Hypothesis*. London: Simon & Schuster Ltd.
6. Nagel, T. (1986). *The View from Nowhere*. New York, NY: Oxford University Press.
7. Bickerton, D. (1995). *Language and Human Behaviour*. Washington: University of Washington Press.
8. Jackendoff, R. (1993). *Patterns in the Mind*. London: Harvester Wheatsheaf.
9. Pinker, S. (1994). *The Language Instinct*. London: Allen Lane, Penguin Press.
10. Fodor, J. A. (1975). *The Language of Thought*. Thomas Y. Crowell Company, Inc.

Chapter 5: The Cognitive Element of Thought

1. Churchland, P. M. (1995). *The Engine of Reason, the Seat of the Soul*. Cambridge, MA: MIT Press.
2. Greenfield, S. A. (1995). *Journey to the Centers of the Mind*. New York, NY: W. H. Freeman & Co.
3. Newman, J., and Baars, B. J. (1993) 'A neural attentional model for access to consciousness: a global workspace perspective'. *Concepts in Neuroscience*, 4(2), 255–290.
4. Barlow, H. (1995). *The Neuron Doctrine in Perception*. Chapter 26: 'The Cognitive Neurosciences'. (Ed. Gazzaniga, M. S.). Cambridge, MA: MIT Press.
5. Freeman, W. J. (1995). *Societies of Brains*. Hillsdale, NJ: Lawrence Erbaum Assocs.
6. Calvin, W. H. (1996). *The Cerebral Code*. Cambridge, MA: MIT Press.
7. Searle, J. R. (1992). *The Rediscovery of the Mind*. Cambridge, MA: MIT Press.

Chapter 6: Thought and Rationality

1. Brown, H. I. (1988). *Rationality*. London: Routledge.
2. Dennett, D. C. (1995). *Darwin's Dangerous Idea*. New York, NY: Simon & Schuster.
3. Mithen, S. (1996). *The Prehistory of the Mind*. London: Thames & Hudson Ltd.
4. Lewontin, R. C. (1991). *The Doctrine of DNA*. London: Penguin Books Ltd.
5. Scruton, R. (1994). *Modern Philosophy*. London: Sinclair-Stevenson.

Chapter 7: Self-awareness and Other Minds

1. Bear, M. F., Connors, B. W., and Paradiso, M. A. (1996). *Neuroscience: Exploring the Brain*. Chapter 14: 'Brain Control of Movement'. Baltimore: Williams & Wilkins.
2. de Bruijn, N. G. (1996). 'Can People Think?' *Journal of Consciousness Studies*, **3**(5–6). Exeter, UK: Imprint Academic.
3. Thorne, K. S. (1994). *Black Holes and Time Warps: Einstein's Outrageous Legacy*. London: Macmillan General Books.

Chapter 8: Consciousness, Self, and Society

1. Baars, B. J. (1988). *A Cognitive Theory of Consciousness*. Cambridge: Cambridge University Press.
2. Penrose, R. (1994). *Shadows of the Mind*. Oxford: Oxford University Press.
3. Goldman-Rakic, P. S. (1995). 'Neurobiology of Mental Representation'. Chapter in: *The Mind, The Brain, and Complex Adaptive Systems* (Ed. Morowitz, H. J. and Singer, J. L.). Reading, MA: Addison-Wesley Publishing Company.
4. Antrobus, J. (1995). *Thinking Away and Ahead. Ibid*.
5. Gazzaniga, M. S. (1995). *Consciousness and the Cerebral Hemispheres*. Chapter 92: 'The Cognitive Neurosciences'. (Ed. Gazzaniga, M. S.). Cambridge, MA: MIT Press.
6. Johnson-Laird, P. N. (1995). *Mental Models, Deductive Reasoning, and the Brain*. Chapter 65. *Ibid*.

Index